lover's guide to palmistry

About the Author

Jon Saint-Germain (Indiana), author of *Karmic Palmistry* and *Runic Palmistry*, decided at age six that he wanted to be a wizard when he grew up. Since then, he has become a professional psychic entertainer, hypnotist, and palm reader with over twenty-five years' experience. He travels around the world giving performances and has even read palms over the radio. In 1997 he was given the Blackwood Award by the Psychic Entertainers Association for his contributions to the literature of mentalism. Jon lives in Bloomington, Indiana, with his wife, Holly, and their two cats.

lover's guide to
palmistry

Finding Love in the Palm of Your Hand

jon saint-germain

Llewellyn Publications
Woodbury, Minnesota

First Edition
First Printing, 2008

Cover illustration © 2008 Rex Bohn/Images.com, cover background and boarder © imagezoo.com
Cover design by Lisa Novak
Editing by Andrea Neff
Interior illustrations by Llewellyn Art Department

Llewellyn is a registered trademark of Llewellyn Worldwide, Ltd.

Library of Congress Cataloging-in-Publication Data
Saint-Germain, Jon.
    Lover's guide to palmistry : finding love in the palm of your hand /
        Jon Saint-Germain.—1st ed.
    p. cm.
    Includes bibliographical references and index.
    ISBN 978-0-7387-1280-2
    1. Palmistry. 2. Love. I. Title.

    BF935.L67S25 2008
    133.6—dc22   2007037082

Llewellyn Publications
A Division of Llewellyn Worldwide, Ltd.
2143 Wooddale Drive, Dept. 978-0-7387-1280-2
Woodbury, Minnesota 55125-2989, U.S.A.
www.llewellyn.com

Printed in the United States of America

Other Books by Jon Saint-Germain

Runic Palmistry
(Llewellyn Publications, 2001)

Karmic Palmistry
(Llewellyn Publications, 2003)

This book is dedicated to Holly, who made me believe in love again.
Without her patience, this book never would have happened.

Contents

Figures

Introduction

In my opinion, the hardest thing we ever learn in life is how to tie our shoes. The rest is all downhill from there.

As we pass through the adventurous and all-too-brief interval between birth and death, we find that few things in life are crystal clear. The universe presents us with an endless series of questions, and rarely are the answers to these questions—especially the truly important ones—easily discovered. The desire to unravel the mysteries of human existence gives birth to all the fields of human endeavor, from the scientific to the occult, from philosophical to spiritual and everything in between. Humans are curious creatures who, when confronted with a puzzle, are willing to exert an infinite amount of time and energy toward finding a solution. Sometimes, if we're both persistent and lucky, we find easy answers. More often we just have to face the unattractive possibility that there are things beyond our understanding that we just have to accept. For some, this idea is intolerable, and so philosophers and theologians are born.

We humans, curious monkeys that we are, seem most fascinated by those questions that arise from our own self-awareness: "Where am I from?" "Where am I going?" "What's my purpose?" "Is there intelligence underlying the universe, or is everything random?"

And probably the most poignant of the imponderable questions: "What would have happened if I had lived my life differently?" If we're hankering to discover a mystery, we don't have to travel to distant lands or faraway galaxies; all we have to do is take a look inside ourselves.

Questions with no real answers are known as imponderables. Philosophers, theologians, and scientists have filled libraries with volumes devoted to speculative thought involving the insolvable riddles of existence. But it becomes clear that, no matter how noble our intentions or how strong our desire to know, no matter how much thought, effort, or debate we bring to these questions, we find ourselves floundering in a sea of ambiguity. If we're not careful, we can drown in that sea and never find answers to anything.

Why do we drive ourselves crazy over questions that may or may not have answers? Because, although we know the answers don't exist in the material world, something within us senses that these are, nonetheless, truly important questions, the answers to which might be found in some inner dimension of personal meaning. Deep down we feel we have a special purpose, a reason for being, a place in the world. We believe that the universe makes sense, even if we can't see the pattern. We second-guess our decisions and torment ourselves over past mistakes. We want a road map to our destiny, and we're willing to pay almost any price for it.

The job of the psychic reader is to explore the nebulous area between the answerable and the imponderable. Weighing and examining possibilities, we help our clients arrive at answers that are meaningful and useful to them. These answers usually are not universal and are, at best, provisional, but nonetheless they can provide a raft for our clients as they cross from one life passage to the next.

There's a famous incident from the life of the Buddha that illustrates the futility of dwelling on irresolvable questions.[1] A chap once asked Lord Buddha a series of such questions, including:

1. Does the Universe have a beginning and end, or no beginning or end?

2. Is there a soul or not, and what happens to it after death if it does exist?

3. Is there a Creator of everything or not?

---

1 This incident is related in the *Majjhima Nikaya Sutta 63: Cula-Malunkyovada Sutta—The Shorter Instructions to Malunkya.*

Lord Buddha (Gautama Siddhartha) lived 2,600 years ago, and these are the very same questions that resist final resolution to this day. We may have beliefs about these abstract issues, but we really don't know the answers, which is why arguments rage and wars are fought over differences of opinion concerning these issues. Lord Buddha answered the questioner in his own inimitable manner, which I will paraphrase:

> It's just as if a man were wounded with an arrow smeared with a deadly poison. His friends and relatives rush to summon a surgeon, but the man says: "I won't have this arrow removed until I know whether the man who wounded me was a warrior, a priest, a merchant, or a worker. I won't have this arrow removed until I know the given name and family name of the man who wounded me; until I know how tall he is; until I know whether he was dark, reddish, or golden-colored; until I know where he's from; until I know whether his bow was a long bow or a crossbow; until I know whether his bowstring was fiber, bamboo threads, sinew, hemp, or bark; until I know what the shaft was made from; until I know whether the feathers of the shaft were those of a vulture, a stork, a hawk, a peacock, or another bird; until I know whether the arrow's shaft was bound with the sinew of an ox, a water buffalo, a mountain cat, or a monkey." The man concluded: "I won't have this arrow removed until I know whether the arrow's shaft was that of a common arrow, a curved arrow, a barbed, a calf-toothed, or an oleander arrow."

That's quite a lengthy monologue for someone lying on the ground, pierced with a poisoned arrow and dying painfully. Yet Buddha pointed out to his persistent questioner that he, the questioner, was in exactly the same condition. He was wagering his life on the answers to questions that could never be answered. Buddha concluded: "The man would die and the answers to all those questions would remain unknown to him."

Wisdom doesn't begin with knowing answers; it begins with recognizing which questions are worth investigating. We'll try to look at some of these questions, and perhaps arrive at answers, as we explore the topics covered in this book.

As a professional palm reader, I'm called upon to practice my craft in a variety of venues. I've appeared everywhere from nine-year-old girls' birthday parties to some of the most exclusive country clubs in my area. My readings at these venues are presented in a lighthearted, entertaining manner. There's a reason for this. It's simply not appropriate, in a party situation, to open emotional wounds. In an entertainment setting, it's better to send people away from the table laughing and with a few new insights, not feeling as though they just engaged in an intense counseling session. But as much as I enjoy the social aspect of parties and special events, the most fascinating aspect of my work, and the most satisfying one, is the private, one-on-one reading. It's also a dangerous, emotionally laden territory, upon which the reader must tread as softly as upon a minefield. An expedition into a person's soul requires respect, knowledge, and delicacy. You never know how an individual will react to a reading. As with walking across a minefield, only an omniscient being can know what step might set off an explosion.

People come to a psychic reader for several reasons. Here are some typical ones:

1. Some people are just curious about psychic matters and are seeking entertainment. I get many phone calls from people who want to drop by with their friends for a quick reading. Usually, they were out driving around talking about psychics, and decided to pick up the phone book and give me a call. These readings, initially embarked upon as a lark, often lead to more private, serious second appointments.

2. Some clients are looking for something to believe in. Surrounded by the constant negativity of the workplace, home, or society in general, some individuals yearn to hear something—anything—positive. They seek something to cling to in the rising swell of negative programming and ever more frightening world events.

3. Most of the time people bring to the table serious emotional issues. These can be anything from self-destructive behavior, a bad marriage, or unhappiness with a job, to the loss of a loved one or dealing with a fatal disease. Usually these clients have already given their situation much thought and may have already sought a solution from more conventional sources, such as friends or professional counselors. Now they want to discuss their issues with someone who can provide an objective and creative point of view. They hope that a psychic can analyze their situation and offer alternative approaches to bring about the outcome they desire.

4. Some people have life situations so tangled and complicated that they need help navigating the situation to arrive at the simplest way to the other end. I happen to be very good at this; it's what I do best. I usually can take the most complex situation and find the simplest through line.

5. Some clients simply are desperate. They've reached the end of their rope and have tried everything they can think of to improve their condition. Often, whether or

not they've been to a psychic before, they believe that we possess some mystical power that can transform their lives for the better. They want a magical solution to their problems. Unfortunately, people who fall into this latter group are at their most vulnerable and are susceptible to psychic frauds. It's also really hard to teach them independence and assertiveness.

6. I have to mention the hard-core skeptic who visits for no other reason than to test the psychic. It's not all that common, but it does happen. It's happened to me three times. Once, a reporter working on an article "exposing" psychic readings as a psychological con game came to me for a reading. I can spot this type very quickly. I brought the session to an end and politely showed her to the door. My advice, for what it's worth, is that you avoid engaging the skeptic in debate. They demand proof but won't accept it when it's given. Nobody wins in this type of argument, and it can lead to a shouting match with nothing ever resolved. I provide a service for people who choose to benefit from it, or entertainment for those who enjoy such things. If a person doesn't fall into one of those two categories, no hard feelings. I can't take this personally; psychic readings aren't for everyone. As my mom used to say, "If everyone liked the same thing, it would be hard to get."

7. Many people simply want fortune-telling ("Is my husband/wife cheating on me?" "How long will I live?" "How many times will I be married?"). Personally, I tend to avoid these types of readings. I believe that the parts of our futures not determined by karma are created, not predicted. Obsessing about predictions that may or may not come true can prevent us from taking responsibility for our own decisions. A theme I constantly harp on throughout my readings is personal responsibility and empowerment.

My suggestion to anyone with a desire to do readings for others is to carefully and honestly examine why you want to do it. What are your motives? It's not our purpose, in my opinion, to be a surrogate parent, no matter how badly some clients want one. Our best and most exciting gift is our ability to give clients information from an alternative point of view. Once we give someone a gift, we can't tell them what to do with it. What they choose to do with that information—apply it, ignore it, or treat it as entertainment—is totally up to them.

Psychic skills are common, although most of us rarely use them in our daily lives. Most people simply don't have a place for intuition or empathy in a world focused on logic and rational thinking. We're encouraged from birth to be rational and to use our heads. This is commendable, but there's more to life than logic. Our minds have an incredible collection of abilities, obscure though some of them may be, that defy logic and reason. These abilities include clairvoyance, psychometry, channeling, and intuition, not to mention the capacity to love.

There's no shortage of opportunities for anyone wishing to learn about psychic matters. All you have to do is peruse any major bookstore to see that people are awakening to their own psychic potential and want to learn more about it. You can learn to read cards, palms, auras, or feet; develop clairvoyance or telekinesis; or speak with deceased loved ones. There's no end to the possibilities.

There are no magical secrets to becoming a psychic counselor. If you've ever loved and lost, and regained the courage to love again; if your heart has been shattered into a million fragments and you still found the courage to keep trying; if you've gone through the dark tunnel of despair and came out the other end, still optimistic, still hopeful, still convinced that life is worth living; if you've looked into the abyss and laughed; if you've seen your dreams crushed into dust, and from that dust new and more resplendent dreams arose, then you already have the heart and soul to be a successful psychic reader. All you need are the tools, which this book will help provide.

There are probably as many reasons that people consult a psychic reader as there are people on the planet. Regardless of the original motives of clients when they first come to me, the reading almost always drifts toward one specific topic, a subject of interest that weaves through the consciousness like a golden thread through an embroidered tapestry. That golden thread is relationships, and the tapestry is the heart.

We all have relationships, whether we want them or not. Even if we're absolutely alone, living in a cave on some distant mountain, we have a relationship with ourselves (actually, this can be the toughest one of all). We're tormented with anxiety, wondering if we'll find happiness with another person. Nothing pulls at my heartstrings more than the plaintive question, "Will I ever find true love?" This book is intended to help the reader answer that question. More importantly, I hope to make clear to the reader that we already possess true love; we just have to learn how to recognize it and express it.

This is the final volume in the trilogy that includes *Runic Palmistry* and *Karmic Palmistry*. The focus of this book is to explore methods of finding the ideal sexual and romantic partner. Nothing comes with a 100 percent guarantee—people are complex and unpredictable—but I truly believe that the information in this book will increase your chances of finding the right person, that special someone with whom you can have a rich, satisfying, and long-term relationship. This belief is based on years of doing readings for people who thought they would never experience romantic happiness, and helping them see that it is indeed possible to find one's soul mate with just a little bit of help. There truly is someone for everybody, if you're willing to look with an open and loving heart.

May the information in this book lead to a deeper understanding of yourself and your potential romantic partner, create a definite picture of what you're looking for in a life mate, and help you find the happiness you deserve. Let's get started.

chapter one

The Riddle of Romance

I have a friend who once remarked, "I don't understand people who commit adultery. A person has his hands full dealing with one relationship. How can anyone juggle two?"

Personally, I think he gives us too much credit. If a person is capable of sustaining *one* relationship, then he or she is well ahead of the game. Let's look at some facts:

Sources such as *Divorce Magazine.com* report that 50 percent of marriages end in divorce. Forty-three percent of marriages are remarriages for at least one partner, proving the old adage that "Hope springs eternal." Sadly, the percentage of remarriages that end in divorce is even higher, around 60 percent.

The message is clear: *we're doing something wrong.* Taking a life mate is one of life's most serious decisions, affecting every aspect of our physical, emotional, and spiritual well-being. A fifty-fifty chance of success is not very encouraging. Would you bet your life on a fifty-fifty chance? If not, why bet your heart? The recent increase in "compatibility finders" and dating services is evidence that we've learned to distrust our hearts, and perhaps with good reason. Unexamined, our feelings can lead us into truly unfortunate situations. For example, if we're driven by the fear of winding up old and alone, we'll almost certainly make bad decisions. It's difficult to make a good decision out of fear.

The Search for the Perfect Mate

Finding that special someone can be a knotty and often frustrating pursuit. We wrack our brains and consume endless books, articles, and television programs looking for new strategies to improve our chances. To add to this dilemma, many of the factors influencing our decisions are hidden from us, pulling our strings and affecting our actions on the subconscious level. In fact, so many subconscious dynamics are at work, involving past experiences, trauma, wishful thinking, and all sorts of other factors, that it's impossible for us to separate free will from internal programming. Sometimes, in order to get the results we want, we just have to hang on and go along for the ride—but perhaps we can gain partial control of the rudder if we're willing to do a little work.

I realize this may be coming across as a little pessimistic, but don't fret—there's hope. Take, for example, couples who have stayed together for decades. We call them "soul mates" and wish that we could be so lucky. But this happy condition didn't happen by accident, fate, or rubbing a lucky rabbit's foot. If we looked at the history of the couple, we'd learn that a lot of work went into polishing off the rough edges that exist even in the best relationships.

Making difficult endeavors appear effortless requires extraordinary skill, and relationships are no exception. Living with another human being can be one of the most stressful situations in life. We have to learn patience, compassion, and generosity. We sometimes have to swallow our pride for the sake of the relationship. Most of all, we have to learn to listen—really *listen*—and true listening isn't done with the ears, but with the heart. In other words, it takes practice.

The Riddle of Attraction

Most of us will have more than one intimate partner during our lifetime; we tend to learn through trial and error. Sometimes our feelings toward someone are so contradictory that even we don't know exactly *why* we find the person attractive. We just know with all our heart that we want him or her. Why are we attracted to one another? What components go into the magnetic appeal we sometimes feel for a person whom we may not even know very well?

If you've studied sociology, you know that scientists have been trying to solve the riddle of relationships for generations. The problem is that human beings are not machines;

we don't always behave according to the rules. An individual is a complex mélange of many factors, including karmic, genetic, and environmental ones. While scientists recognize the formative influence of genetics and environment, most have yet to recognize the existence of karma. And yet karma may be one of the most important factors determining the circumstances of our birth, basic personality pattern, and, consequently, the person we consider our perfect mate. Why we're attracted to a certain individual is a manifestation of all these factors: genetic, environmental, and karmic.

Many scientists believe that humans are biologically programmed to seek out a romantic relationship with one special and unique person. Some studies seem to suggest that love is not merely an emotional feeling related to happiness, but a primal force more akin to lust or hunger. We fall in love based on that swept-away feeling, which can be just as powerful for someone we've just met as for someone we've known for years. This can happen at any time: at work, while out to dinner with friends, or when meeting someone through a singles ad in the newspaper. Eyes lock, breathing becomes husky, magic happens. We have met THE ONE.

Regardless of the circumstances that bring two people together, the bottom line is the same: we have a powerful urge to mate with one person, excluding all others, and we're more than willing to suffer all manner of difficulties to satisfy this urge.

The Pink Lens Effect

There's usually a period of idealism at the beginning of each new relationship. New lovers romanticize their partner, magnifying the good points and brushing away the flaws. This is sometimes called the "pink lens effect," which can be completely out of sync with the perceptions of outsiders. "What in the world does she see in *him*?" they ask. This is the question we've been trying to answer since man and woman first looked at each other. What do we see in each other?

A relatively recent development in relationships is the "Internet romance" often experienced by people who spend a lot of time in Internet chat rooms and forums. The Internet relationship is so new that we really haven't been able to study it in-depth, but it is, in my opinion, a fascinating phenomenon.

I know people who have met the love of their life this way; others tell horror stories about predators and stalkers. It behooves a person to be careful when meeting other people, no matter what the circumstances—they are not always what they pretend to be. One disadvantage of an Internet relationship is that we don't know who or what is on the other end of the computer: all we know is these words magically appear on our screen in response to what we type in. On the other hand, the long-distance, getting-to-know-each-other process seems to add a strong intensity to the relationship often missing in modern romance. When we meet someone in person and experience a strong mutual attraction, we sometimes hasten through the preliminaries in order to satisfy the physical cravings of sexual desire.

The Internet, however, seems to take the place of the nineteenth-century chaperone who used to oversee the interactions of a young couple so they wouldn't succumb to lustful improprieties. The potential companions communicating through the Internet have to take their time and get to know each other. If the two are mutually compatible and attracted to each other, this can create an intense longing to meet in person. When the meeting occurs, the romance, so long deferred, experiences momentum as though shot from a cannon. Another danger I've seen is the substitution of a fantasy-based Internet relationship for a real, interactive, up-close-and-personal relationship with a flesh and blood person. Many people fear relationships, are afraid of being hurt, but nonetheless yearn for the intimacy of a romance without the danger. This is a real danger of the Internet relationship: hiding behind the anonymity of the computer and never, ever taking the emotional gamble of meeting in person.

As my dad used to point out, young people think they invented love. Newly bonded couples love to exalt the relationship. New lovers are sure that their relationship is more special and beautiful than anyone else's. Unfortunately for the myth of "eternal love" so exalted in music and other media, this pink lens effect wears off over time. Boundaries drop, and the two individuals, who once were halves of a perfect whole, discover that they are, in fact, completely different individuals. Some hand types, such as air, which are known for being eternally idealistic, tend to fall in love with the perceived image of the person, an ideal created in the mind, rather than based on experience with the actual person. They project a fantasy of who they want the person to be over the real person. Eventually, when the illusion fades, there is mutual disillusionment. The two scramble to regain what they thought they already had. This can be a rocky period for all couples, as each partner vies for his or her position within the relationship.

Addicted to Love

Biologists have discovered that infatuation creates chemical states in the brain similar to those created by addictive drugs. This explains that ecstatic feeling when we first fall in love. Falling in love produces a tremendous upsurge of dopamine and norephedrine—exactly the same chemical cocktail produced by mood-altering drugs.

When we compare love to a drug addiction, we understand how our need to mate often overrides our common sense. As with any drug, there comes a point when the body adjusts to it, and we immediately want more of it. The effect wears off and we mourn for what we once possessed. There's little wonder that so many people become relationship junkies, going from one relationship to the next. They're trying to make permanent that natural "high" felt at the beginning of a love affair.

Beginnings Lead to Endings

All relationships end. This is a fact of life, inescapable and as certain as the pull of gravity on solid objects. Even if we beat the odds and succeed in a lifelong relationship, the death of either partner brings separation. We hate to acknowledge this, preferring to believe that we'll be together forever with our beloved. Deep in our hearts, we yearn for permanent, unchanging romantic bliss. Because we wish that happy state could last forever, any change in the relationship threatens us. We fear change, feeling that any alteration in the existing balance presages disaster. Dissatisfaction and fear take root. "You're not the same person you used to be!" we cry. Yes, true—but who is? We change moment to moment, not to mention year to year.

Every relationship has to run its course, whether it lasts a few minutes or an entire lifetime. If the relationship is long-term, it doesn't take a geologist to predict that there will be peaks and valleys. In a relationship lasting several years it's only natural that both partners will change. Sometimes these changes lead to a closer bond. Sometimes the partners grow apart from each other. Like carriages drawn by horses in different directions, the two proceed toward individual destinations. The more we try to hang on to a situation, to capture it in our hands, the more elusive the situation becomes. Sometimes we just have to let go. Resisting change is like trying to stop winter by looking at pictures of the beach. Once we realize that everything in the world is impermanent and subject to change, relationships become less stressful. We learn to let go of fear, to relax and enjoy each moment together.

Just because a relationship ends doesn't mean it was a failure. Each relationship is an adventure that teaches us to expand our personal boundaries, explore the needs of our heart, and gain a better understanding of our inner workings.

My Ego Is Bigger Than Your Ego

I admit it—I'm a romantic. I cling to the belief that anybody can learn to get along with anyone else if the motivation to do so can be found. I believe this even though the world is torn apart by wars and conflicts of every description. I believe, from the bottom of my heart, that people are essentially good and that this goodness will manifest if given a chance. Whether my belief in this matter is in accordance with the real world or not, it helps me sleep better at night. I seriously believe that we all can learn to live with each other in peace.

I think the main thing that prevents us from getting along with one another is our own selfish ego. The ego is like a child screaming for attention. It loves to be in control, resists change, and hates to be refused anything. Problems arise when this determination to always be right, to always be in control, drives a wedge between people and between nations. "My God is superior to your God," "Our political structure is better than your political structure," "My way of doing things is better than your way of doing things." From this constant belief in our own "rightness," conflicts erupt.

Left untended, conflict always grows. We've all seen the tragedies resulting from conflict escalating out of control, both on a personal level and worldwide. Within a relationship, the simplest conflict, left unaddressed, can escalate until it blows the relationship apart.

One ego in conflict with another is a distressing thing to witness, but it seldom ends there. There's a ripple effect that pulls in more and more people. To nip it in the bud, we have to recognize that when we fall in love with our own views so completely that we'll do anything to defend them, there can be harmful—even disastrous—consequences. We must realize that just because we believe something strongly doesn't make it ultimate truth, and just because we want something very badly doesn't mean it's natural law that we should get it. A fight doesn't begin with the first blow; it begins with the second. Taming the ego is the first step toward real maturity. A tamed ego doesn't look for a fight. A tamed ego walks away from conflict. The ability to cool the ego enough to walk away from a fight is a significant sign of maturity—and also, unfortunately, a rare one.

In any relationship, whether between individuals or nations, the defining characteristics are tolerance and appreciation for each other's differences. If we force our beliefs on another, this is an act of violence. Attempting to control or change another person is another act of violence, one that creates resistance. It's saying, in effect, "Who you are isn't as satisfactory as the way I want you to be. You have to change to make me happy." To be happy and fulfilled, people must have the freedom to follow their own path. This is what makes life such a fascinating adventure, and the adventure is much more fun when you're holding someone's hand as you go.

The Secrets to Success

People come to my sanctum sanctorum (or send me pictures of their hands) asking, "Are we compatible with each other?" This is a very complicated question, depending on the dynamics of each individual case. If palmistry teaches us anything, it's that people are not easily lumped into predictable categories. Individuals are volatile, flexible, and full of surprises. Good people sometimes do bad things, and even the most evil people have aspects of tenderness and generosity. If we react to a specific event one way today, we may react to it differently tomorrow. We learn from experience and modify our strategies. We weigh, scrutinize, and alter our interactions constantly. This adaptability is one of our greatest tools. Even if we can't change our circumstances, we can always change how we react to them. This gives us a tremendous amount of power. We can make ourselves into whatever we want to be. Therefore, compatibility is definitely a factor that is under our control, at least to some extent. It doesn't necessarily have to happen through some divine magic.

Not all relationships are salvageable, and some of them, sadly, don't need to be saved—they need to be terminated before someone gets hurt. More often than I would like, I see clients who are in an abusive relationship. I've learned that this kind of relationship isn't a phenomenon of the lower economic demographic, but rather it spans all social and economic strata. I've probably seen more clients from upper-income families in abusive relationships than from lower-income families. My goal is to help them get out of this nightmare and into some intense therapy. Nobody should stay in an abusive relationship for one moment. However, there seems to be an addictive quality to these relationships that's difficult to break. Statistics show that only half of the women who stay with an abusive spouse do so for financial reasons. Many stay out of love, pity, guilt, denial, sympathy for their spouse's "sickness," optimism that the abusive behavior will change, and so on. In fact, my mother, who was an excellent astrologer, retired from her practice over this very issue. When I asked her why she quit doing readings, she told me she was tired of people not listening to her when she told them to get out of a bad relationship. My mother's control issues aside, when I recognize that my client is suffering from the abuse of his or her mate, I refer the person to one of the many social agencies in my area that specialize in this terrible affliction.

Palmistry is as much an art as a science. Later on, we'll see that classical palmistry teaches that a fire person doesn't relate well to a water person. Although this is a good general rule, I've seen fire/water matings—and other combinations of "antagonistic elements"—succeed. The secret to their success is simple: Each partner respects the other's differences and is willing to adapt his or her own behaviors to accommodate the other. They don't try to mold or change each other. Neither partner has to always be right or be in control. There is compromise, empathy, and trust. Both partners have room to breathe. I have to say that, sadly, these relationships are exceptions rather than the rule. I refer you to the divorce statistics cited at the beginning of this chapter for proof.

Successful couples learn that there's more to a loving relationship than the satisfaction of needs. For the good of the relationship, we have to adapt to changing circumstances and let go of our selfishness. This level of understanding comes with trial and error, learning what does and doesn't work for us. To truly enjoy the rewards of a deep, satisfying relationship, we have to work at it. If everyone devoted as much time and effort to building relationship skills as they do to learning jobs skills, the world would be a much calmer place in which to live.

Even if we're willing to put in the study and practice necessary to master the skills of relationship building, we still can benefit from some help to lessen the learning curve. To a couple wanting to know more about compatibility, palmistry is most valuable in identifying differences in personality that can lead to predictable conflicts. We can identify areas of the relationship that need extra work, and define reasonable boundaries based on each partner's needs and ability to contribute to the relationship.

Palmistry is meant to be used as a guideline, not a rule. I would be reluctant to advise a couple with loving feelings for each other to break up because of something I see in their hands. For me to do so would be inexcusably arrogant. However, I can point out areas of potential conflict and help the couple find ways around the problems. This is significant because little things, quirky peccadillos or minor character flaws that seem inconsequential at the beginning of a new relationship, can build and grow over time to monolithic proportions. It's hard for us to see undesirable traits in ourselves because it's impossible to be objective about our own lives. Sometimes we all need an outside point of view to help us see more clearly what we need to do in order to get what we want.

And that, in a nutshell, is my job.

Let's take a look at what we can learn from the hands.

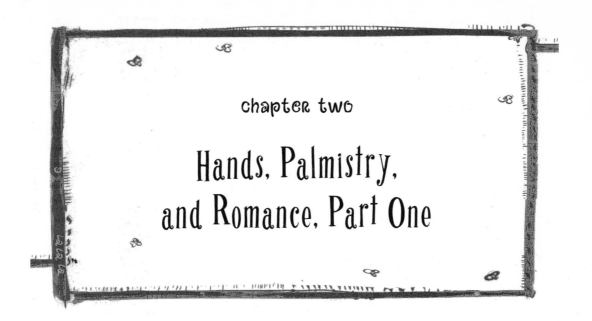

chapter two

Hands, Palmistry, and Romance, Part One

The human hand is a fascinating, complex, and precise piece of machinery that has been refined through the process of evolution into the shape it is today. In evolutionary terms, the hand started out as a mitten-like flipper (a five-fingered bone structure is still found in the flippers of whales and dolphins), developed into a primitive claw structure in the early primates, and finally evolved into the precise manipulative tool we have today. When we examine our hands, we're peering into the very essence of human evolution from primordial times to the present. Right at the end of our arm is the pinnacle of nature's art, the device that gave us the edge over every other creature in existence and allowed us to dominate the Earth and shape it to our will.

You don't have to be an expert hand reader to gather a few Cheirological first impressions from someone's hands. After all, conventional wisdom contains many choice bits of common knowledge concerning our hands. For example, the relative firmness of the hand can provide loads of information. Thin, flabby hands are more likely to belong to individuals who lack stamina and energy and avoid strong emotions of any kind, whether pleasant or unpleasant. Large, flabby hands, especially if warm to the touch, can indicate a sensualist, a person who may overindulge in food, sex, and, in some cases, drugs and alcohol. A warm, firm handshake generally is considered a sign of good character. A considerate person takes care to adjust the pressure of his or her handshake to accommodate the person with whom he or she is shaking hands. However, if the person attempts to crush your hand during a friendly handshake, then you know you're dealing with an aggressive, competitive personality. He or she always will try to get the "upper hand." Sweaty hands denote nervousness, unless the individual suffers from a medical condition called *hyperhidrosis*, which causes excessive sweating of the palms of the hand. An almost instantaneous shift in hand moisture is one of the major factors measured in lie-detector tests. It's called the galvanic skin response, and is a good indicator of nervousness or guilt.

Warm hands have good circulation and indicate a relaxed, confident attitude. A cold hand can indicate stress. Someone with a weak, flabby grip obviously lacks vitality and energy. If a person uses sweeping, vigorous gestures while he or she speaks, you can bet on an extroverted, passionate personality. Tightly controlled gestures that stay close to the body indicate a person who tries to maintain control over his or her emotions at all times.

Furthermore, the days have passed when hand lotion and fingernail polish were solely the domain of women. An assortment of skin and nail care products for men are now available. So if you're on a first date with a guy and notice that he has manicured nails and moist, lotioned hands, he's going to have a different self-image than a chap with calloused hands and chipped nails.

Whether the hands are big or small can reveal a lot about the person's outlook. The span of an average hand is the distance from the tip of the chin to about halfway between the eyebrows and the hairline. Try it yourself to get the feel for it. Rest the bottom edge of your palm near the wrist on the bottom edge of your chin, and see how far the fingers reach. If your hand doesn't make it much past the eyebrows, it's considered a small hand. If it reaches all the way to your hairline or even higher, then your hand is considered large.

Here is what we learn from this exercise: Small hands usually belong to people who are more in tune with the *overview* of a situation. They can see the big picture. Large hands indicate an ability to multitask, to deal with many things simultaneously on a very detailed level. An average-sized hand reveals equanimity. The individual will have a balanced approach to life, neither too picky nor too liberal, with the ability to set numerous goals and achieve most of them.

Not bad, eh? Even if you know nothing about palm reading, look how much you can learn just from a casual examination of a stranger's hands. In my personal practice, I find the cold hand "tell" very useful in determining if the client is relaxed and confident in the situation or nervous and apprehensive. In the event that the client is nervous, I begin the reading in a nonthreatening and pleasant manner, with the intention of making the client more relaxed. I assure the person, "Nothing that I'm going to tell you today will be scary or cause you anxiety. I haven't lost a patient yet." I also press firmly and discreetly on the hollow between the first and second fingers' knuckles, a reflexology trick that induces relaxation.

And let's not overlook the role that hands play in romantic rituals. Experts in body language tell us a common flirtation behavior is called "palming." When people of either sex observe that they're being watched by a potential romantic partner, they're likely to respond with seemingly idle grooming motions, such as smoothing their hair, shirt, or blouse, straightening their tie, or picking at imaginary lint. Interestingly enough, the more palm area the person exposes during these gestures, the more interested he or she is in the attention being shown. It's also interesting to notice that this behavior is common even in primates such as chimpanzees and gorillas. In a more intimate setting, the hands are used to fondle and caress our lover. The palm of the hand is a very intimate area, rich in nerve endings. We hold hands with our beloved to affirm our close bond, and a light tickling or kissing of the palm can be quite erotic.

The palms of our hands reveal us at our most vulnerable. When threatened, we often cross our arms in front of us, protecting both the heart chakra and the palms of our hands. When we yield ourselves to another, we expose the palms of our hands to the person, a very trusting gesture. This is why it's a good idea to respect this trust when reading someone else's palm. Quite often, a new client is reluctant to open his or her hand all the way. The client extends his or her hand with the fingers protectively curled over the palm. Sometimes I have to gently coax the hand open in order to give a reading.

Which Hand to Read?

A palm reader will hear this question almost every time he or she begins a reading. The quick answer is that, to do a thorough job, you should look at both hands. However, for a fast reading, you will want to concentrate on the dominant hand. On a right-handed person, the left hand is considered the hand of past influences and the right hand represents the present circumstances, although a few palmists recently have questioned this assumption, claiming that information is equally distributed across both hands.

When we are born, both hands are very similar. As we mature, the dominant hand changes faster, acting as the agent of our thoughts and desires. We write, eat, defend ourselves, and caress our loved ones with this hand. As we react to the world and as our personality develops, the dominant hand records these changes. The passive hand evolves, too, but at a much slower rate. This is why classical palmists say the right hand represents the present and the left hand represents the past. Some schools consider the left hand the repository of past-life information and karmic issues that we bring into this life at birth.

The Elements of Romance

People tend to fall into basic categories of behavior, and a tool that allows quick identification of these categories is a very handy thing to have. As I've mentioned in my previous writings, I have a great fondness for the method of classifying hands into the elements *earth, air, fire,* and *water.* In addition to the four classical elements, I include two other important elements from traditional Chinese hand reading, *wood* and *metal.* In traditional Chinese divination, the five elements are *earth, water, wood, metal,* and *fire*—no air element ever is included. However, air is included in the Vedic concept of *dhatus,* a model that suggests human beings consist of earth (solid), water (liquid), fire (heat), and air (breath and sometimes spirit). These elements, or dhatus, can be used to describe physical qualities, personality types, and health issues. They also can give us a window into the primal, instinctive part of our nature.

Academic interest aside, why is this important? What do we care about what element our hands fall into? In palmistry, we attempt to grasp the gestalt of a person's individuality. By looking at the hands, we try to tune in to the very essence of a person. How we conduct ourselves, the choices we make, and our reactions to various stimuli are largely instinctive. Under pressure, we seldom take time to analyze our feelings. We respond spontaneously and instinctively to the situation in which we find ourselves. In classical palmistry, the element representing our hand describes our instinctive approach to life, the "bottom line" of an individual's personality. In this chapter, we'll learn how to determine which element various hands fall into, the characteristics of each element, and the romantic and emotional "flavor" of each element. Furthermore, the categories of antagonistic and complementary elements play an important role in the compatibility profiles I've compiled in chapter 6.

Categorizing a hand is not as simple as it seems at first glance. Although there are only six elemental types, many people don't fall neatly into any one elemental category. If they did, our job would be much easier. Most people have traces of several elements, some people blend two elements, and a rare few individuals are pure examples of a single element. Typically, you'll find that the fingers are one type and the palm another.

Adding to this complexity is the fact that some people will exhibit different elements in the right and left hands. In this case, the dominant hand reveals our social element: who we are at the present time, based on whatever social and emotional experiences we've had over the course of a lifetime. The subdominant hand represents the far past, being very close to the hand we brought to this life from birth. In the subdominant hand, we find the primordial roots of the person: genetic and karmic influences, before the pressures of family and society began to shape us. When using palmistry to learn about a potential lover, I think it's more important to understand who the person is in the present time, regardless of past influences. Then, as you get to know the person better, take a look at his or her past influences. For now, we'll focus our attention on the dominant hand.

Even with hands combining two or more elements, it's possible to categorize the hand by a single element by determining which type the subject's hand resembles most after eliminating weaker elements. Some elements are subordinate to others. The rules to remember are as follows:

Wood conquers earth

Earth conquers water

Water conquers fire

Fire conquers metal

Metal conquers wood (think of an ax felling a tree)

Air conquers all

Therefore:

- Earth and fire are complementary

- Earth and water are complementary

- Fire and air are complementary

- Earth and air are antagonistic

- Water and air are antagonistic

- Fire and water are antagonistic

And among the rarer elements:

- Metal and water are complementary

- Metal and earth are complementary

- Metal and air are antagonistic

- Metal and fire are antagonistic

- Wood and water are complementary

- Wood and earth are complementary

- Wood and air are complementary

- Wood and fire are antagonistic

- Wood and metal are antagonistic

- Metal and fire are antagonistic

Therefore, if we're really stumped by a certain hand combining mixed elements, we at least can arrive at a beginning point through the elimination of weaker elements. For example, if a hand is a fire/water mixture, then we can call it a water hand, since water conquers fire. An earth/water mixture is an earth type, since earth conquers water. In more advanced practice, it's a little more complicated than that, but this is a good general rule of thumb for a quick analysis.

Measuring the Finger/Palm Ratio

Hand types typically are defined by the ratio of the lengths of the fingers to the dimensions of the palm. The palm represents the unconscious instincts, while the fingers represent how these instinctive urges are manifested in the real world. Together, they reveal who we are on the inside, and what aspects of ourselves we choose to show the world.

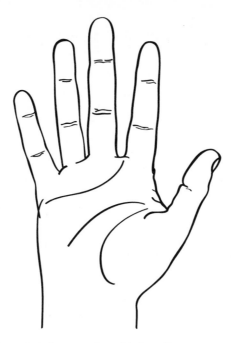

Figure 2-1: Square palm with long fingers

The first technique we'll learn is how to determine if the hand has a square or rect-angular palm. A square palm is close to the same length at its longest point as it is at its broadest point (Figure 2-1).

If the palm is noticeably longer in either direction, it's rectangular. You can use a ruler or caliper to determine this ratio, if you'd like.

Determining finger length is a little trickier. Some palmists have a knack for gauging finger length at a glance. If this is a problem for you (and it is, sometimes, for me), there are many ways to do this other than by visual inspection. Again, you'll find a ruler or caliper useful. Long fingers are almost as long as the palm is wide, and short fingers fall shorter than the palm's width. Obviously, the hand print shown in figure 2-1 has long fingers, while figure 2-2 shows a person with short fingers.

The long and short ratio is relative. A person can have long fingers compared to some-one with shorter fingers, yet in the palm/finger ratio the fingers still are considered short. Therefore, it's a good idea to have a scientific approach in your bag of tricks. The most

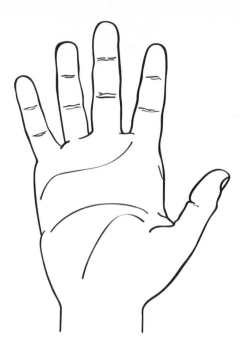

Figure 2-2: Short fingers

practical method is one suggested by Fred Gettings in *The Book of the Hand*. You'll need a compass used by draftsmen to draw circles, some ink and paper, and a hand to measure.

It's really helpful to make a print of the hand. If you're working in a venue where you don't have time to make prints, such as a psychic fair or house party, there's another method, which I'll describe shortly. But for now, let's assume that we have all the time we need. Place the point of the compass at the base of the second finger (the finger of Saturn) and adjust it so that the radius is the tip of the second finger.

Now, using the base of the second finger as the center, draw a complete circle. If the circle encompasses most of the hand, including the thumb, then the fingers are long (figure 2-3). If the circle falls well within the area of the palm and misses the tip of the thumb, then the fingers are short (figure 2-4). Obviously, there will be a lot of variation from hand to hand, but this method usually is quite reliable.

If you're not working from a print, you can use my "finger compass" method. Place the tip of your thumb at the base of the middle finger and the tip of your forefinger at the tip of the middle finger. Keeping your thumb firmly in place and using the forefinger

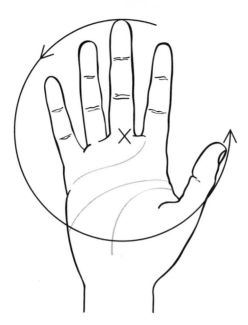

Figure 2-3: Radius of long fingers

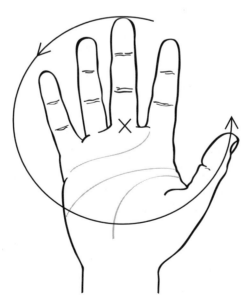

Figure 2-4: Radius of short fingers

as a compass, swing your forefinger around in a circle, taking care not to alter the distance between it and your thumb. Mentally visualize the circle and make your determinations. With practice, this method works almost as well as the Gettings method. Now that we know how to determine whether the palm is square or rectangular, and if the fingers are long or short, let's see what we can do with this information.

Your Lover in a Nutshell

Let's take a look at the basic personality expressions for each of the elements according to hand type. This is our first overview of hand interpretation, and the general profile will become refined and modified by other factors, such as finger ratios, hand lines, and other items of interest, all of which we'll discuss later in this book.

Earth Hand

The earth hand (figure 2-5) is usually the easiest of the four types to recognize. The qualities to look for are a square, meaty palm, short fingers, and very few lines. The few lines found in the palm reflect a preference for simplicity. If the fingers are rounded at the tips, the person may be a bit impatient. In an intimate setting, these people may have to learn to slow down and wait for their partner's signals to proceed to the next level. Square tips suggest an individual who thinks a bit more before acting, so often these people are more interested—sometimes a *lot* more interested—in a potential romantic partner than they let on.

Think of the Earth itself when you see this hand. Mountains and trees tend to be stable and solidly rooted, and they move slowly. The Earth is fertile, so this hand reveals an active interest in sex. Although earth types usually aren't the most passionate romantics, they are nurturing and supportive. For the person with an earth hand, relationships do not burn like fire, nor do they flow like water, but are sources of security and stability.

You have to be careful not to mistake this hand type for the metal hand, which has a square palm and square fingers and is harder to the touch than the earth hand. The earth hand is similar to what is called the *practical hand* in classical palmistry.

The subject possessing an earth hand will be practical, down-to-earth (naturally), reliable, predictable, emotionally stable, and often conservative. The line patterns of these hands are usually very simple, reflecting the person's simple and direct approach to life.

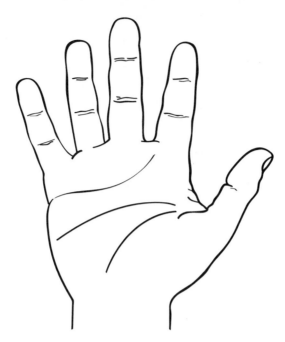

Figure 2-5: Earth hand

Earth types tend to examine a potential partner from a practical point of view: Will he or she be a good provider? A good partner? Good with children? Reliable in a pinch?

The earth hand denotes individuals who are fond of tradition, even if it's a tradition they invented themselves. Their motto is "If it isn't broke, don't fix it," so once they find a romantic partner with whom they're comfortable, they're as loyal as a bulldog. Sometimes they have to be encouraged to try new techniques in the bedroom, as once they find something they like, they tend to stick with it. Typically, they resist change and are slow to experiment with novel procedures. In answer to the question, "If you don't try it, how do you know you don't like it?" the earth type will respond, "I just do."

People with earth hands possess a strong work ethic, are punctual, and tend to provide for the future. They neither lead nor follow, preferring to do things their own way in their own time. It's important to give them their space and not crowd them.

Earth types have to learn to open themselves to new experiences. They loath complexity, so tangled emotional issues make them uncomfortable. In a complicated emotional situation, they tend to practice avoidance, hoping the conflict will pass away.

The romantic style of earth types is sentimental, methodical, and caring. They remember birthdays, anniversaries, and even the day the two of you met. Sentimental and protective, they make excellent parents. As lovers, they are eager to please and will exert a lot of effort toward pleasuring their partner. Sometimes they enjoy foreplay more than sexual intercourse itself, prefacing the romantic interlude with a back or foot massage. Gentle, affectionate cuddling leads to caressing and smoothly segues into foreplay. They can be sneaky this way. Remember that earth types build their foundations one brick at a time, working step by step toward their ultimate goal. They should look for their ideal romantic partner among other earth types, wood types, and sometimes the more stable water types. They don't do well with fire types, as the emotional intensity can scorch them. Also, earth types seem a bit boring and restrictive to the intense fire type.

Fire Hand

The fire hand (figure 2-6) has short fingers, denoting impatience, and a long palm, indicating the owner's vast reserves of emotional, nervous, and physical energy. The fire hand is usually hot to the touch. People with this hand type are passionate and intense. They love change and variety and become bored easily. They hate restrictions, limitations, or falling into a rut.

A person with a fire hand possesses strong desires, appetites, and ambition. Great starters, they seldom finish their projects, especially if the work takes too long. Consequently, when younger or otherwise lacking in self-awareness, they can go through relationships like other people go through socks. They become enamored with a person, but over time they can lose interest and move on to someone new and novel. Boredom sets in if something takes too long before the payoff, and this includes relationships.

Fire is ambitious, and if the fire element is too strong, it can lead to domineering behavior both in the workplace and within a relationship. A fire hand with a tempering element of earth or water is ideal. Fire types have to be mindful of how their actions affect others; otherwise, their ambition can cause them to run over other people on the way to their goal. Since fire can burn only so long, they risk burnout, not only on the job but in their personal relationships. Always on the go, experimental, and in love with variety, fire type are very difficult to keep up with.

Fire types should seek their mates among other fire types who share similar goals, or among the imaginative air types, whom they see as a constant source of stimulation. Water isn't a fortunate element for them, as water smothers fire.

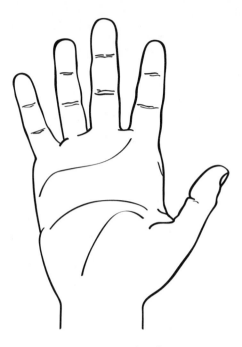

Figure 2-6: Fire hand

The romantic style of a fire type is passionate, mercurial, and often possessive. Fire types must learn to relax control and use power wisely. In a relationship, they often will parlay for control over money, location of living quarters, who initiates sex, where to go out to eat, and so on. People with fire hands can be sexually insatiable when aroused. During lovemaking, their passion is fanned to an inferno, and the sexual experience is breathtaking, fierce, galvanic, and exhausting.

Fire types don't want to accept the imperfections of the world, and they constantly try to improve what they find, by their standards, unsatisfactory. Unfortunately, this can lead to difficulties in relaxing and enjoying what they already have, especially in relationships.

Air Hand

Recognizable by its short, square palm and long fingers, the air hand (figure 2-7) denotes a person with a quick, agile mind. The negative side of the air type is a tendency to deceive and manipulate. Air types are great self-motivators and work according to their

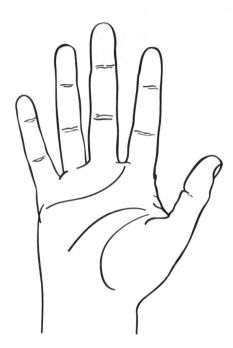

Figure 2-7: Air hand

own inner agenda. They tend to be independent, often resent the controlling influence of authority, and respond readily to new ideas. They can be a bit flamboyant in their behavior, sometimes acting in a contrived manner to elicit a desired response from others. Consequently, they don't always mean what they say.

Natural entertainers, air types enjoy attention and recognition. They are so versatile and multifaceted that it is as though there are several different people living in their heads. Being involved with an air type is like dating four or five different people. In a relationship, they alternate between a needy state, hungry for touch and reassurance, and an isolated state, craving solitude to introspect and collect their thoughts.

Naturally explorative and curious, an air type will try anything at least once. These people are great at debate and often will argue either side of an issue just for the fun of it. Consequently, domestic squabbles often remain unresolved, veering off on tangents and into non sequiturs. Air types enjoy psychology and playing mind games, with themselves as well as others, so sometimes they see a domestic dispute as a fertile field for exploring intellectual concepts. When an air type responds with this intellectual detachment to the owner of one of the more practical elements, such as earth or metal, the earth or metal type becomes furious.

People with air hands are usually two steps ahead in a situation, because before entering a new job or social situation or going on a date, they've already rehearsed several possible scenarios in their mind and formulated responses to the events most likely to transpire.

People with the air hand are very good at generating concepts, theories, and ideas, although they seldom find the time to act on all of them. Air types have a dry sense of humor and are notorious practical jokers, so life with them is never dull.

Air types should find their mates among other air types or among fire types, as long as they take care to not let the fire type burn them out. Air types sometimes feel restricted and limited in a relationship with the more conventional earth types.

The romantic style of people with air hands is idealistic, dramatic, and fun-loving. Some of the more manipulative air types will say anything to get what they want, so sometimes they're not as sincere about their feelings as they sound. This isn't always the case; just watch out for it. They adore role-playing and romantic fantasies, so air is easily one of the "kinkiest" of the elemental types, integrating fantasy and imagination into their lovemaking. They enjoy costuming in the bedroom and playing out erotic scenarios.

Air types tend to fall in love with their perceived image of a person, created in their mind, rather than based on interaction with the actual person. It's as though they project a fantasy of who they want the person to be over the real person. Eventually, when the illusion fades, there can be great disappointment. When they're making love to you, you sometimes wonder who they're with inside their head. You can see them drift off into their fantasy world and may have to remind them, "Hey! I'm right here."

The air type, by the way, is my ideal lover.

Water Hand

A water hand (figure 2-8) has a rectangular palm with many fine lines, is very soft and flexible, and is topped off with long, smoothly tapered fingers. Water is the most flexible and unstable of the four elements. Earth is always earth, and fire is always fire, but water can be liquid, solid, or gaseous. Water can assume the states of the other three elements as well as its own. Therefore, the water type tends to be moody, and at times their external appearance is completely at odds with the internal reality. "You can't judge a book by its cover" is definitely true of a water type. Water often is plagued by mood swings and conflicting impulses, as it shifts from a solid (earthlike) state, through a liquid one (water),

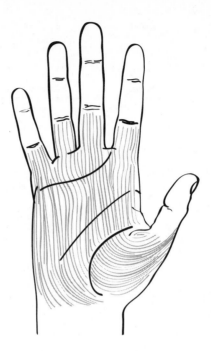

Figure 2-8: Water hand

and finally to a gaseous (airlike) state. The long fingers denote perfectionism and sensitivity to detail. Because of the myriad tiny lines covering the surface, water hands tend to look old. However, the lines have nothing to do with age but rather are an indication of the intensity of the person's emotional expression. It's difficult to read a water type's moods from his or her face, as "still waters run deep." These people are watchers and observers. This holds true especially if the fingers are knobby. Visual stimulation is particularly arousing to them.

Water types are restless. They need a grounding influence or else they'll tend to scatter their energy all over the place. They approach subjects indirectly and can talk for hours about nothing in particular. However, when grounded by a solid relationship, they reach equilibrium and can be tremendously productive and creative. Because they love to approach a subject from various interesting angles, water types have unique perspectives and their own way of doing things, so in a relationship they throw out established rules and make it up as they go along.

Water types tend to be sensitive to criticism and can feel rejection where none is intended, so they need encouragement and support. On the other hand, they can be quite intuitive, and their first impression of people is often right on target.

Water types should seek their mates among other water types, wood types, or the less-restricted members of the earth type, as the secure boundaries of earth help contain the restless water element. Water and fire can work together in business with powerful results (and sex between a fire and water type can be "steamy"!), but for a long-term relationship the mixture is usually too volatile. The fire type eventually will feel drowned by the water element, and the water's emotional vitality will be "evaporated" by the fire.

Since water types have a tendency to scatter their energy all over the place, the romantic challenge for them is to find a suitable channel for their flowing energy, directing the wellsprings of their emotion into a useful and productive relationship. They have to let go of piddly drains on their attention and learn to stay focused on the truly important things.

The romantic style of water is caring, nurturing, and responsible. Love at first sight is dangerous for water types, since their hearts are sensitive to a person in pain or possessed of complicated emotional issues. If you happen to have a water hand, and you experience love at first sight while looking across a room full of strangers—RUN! Water types are prone to parent/child relationships, with the water person as the parent and the partner in the child role. These relationships almost always fall apart due to the stresses of the dependency issues. When the "child" matures, he or she has a natural desire to leave the nest.

Making love with a water type is a deep, emotionally absorbing experience. With their empathy, water types can find all the right buttons to push, physically and emotionally. They can open you up so completely that when you climax, you find all your emotions pouring out alongside your pleasure like a jet of water blasting through a breach in a dam. It's not uncommon to find yourself having a cleansing cry after making love with a water type.

Wood Hand

A wood hand (figure 2-9) has gnarled, knobby knuckles and thin fingers with fine vertical lines. Usually, the bones and tendons are prominent. This hand type is sometimes known in Western palmistry as the *philosophic hand*.

Wood types are thinkers, and are very facile with complex ideas and abstract thought. They adore psychology, philosophy, and theories of human behavior. Over time, they

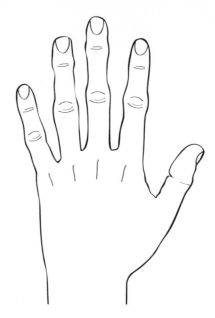

Figure 2-9: Wood hand

develop their own spirituality, picking and choosing elements from several schools of thought to forge a spiritual fusion entirely their own. People with wood hands love conversation and discussion and are usually good at debate, which they conduct logically and passionately. They also know amazing amounts of trivia and obscure information. Wood hands often are found on carpenters, craftsmen, and other people who have skilled hands. They tend to be physically active and have a broad outlook on life. Wood types frequently are disappointed by the shortcomings of others, but more so by their own failures to maintain the high standards to which they aspire. This is a trait that wood shares with air.

Wood types make good teachers and lecturers, but have to be careful not to get lost in endless speculation and elegant theories that look good on paper but have no practical value. This teaching aspect can manifest within a sexual relationship, wherein they like nothing better than to assume an instructor role and school their students/lovers in various exotic sexual techniques, often drawn from tantric yoga and the *Kama Sutra*.

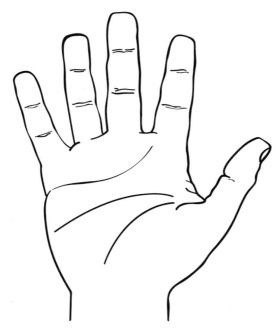

Figure 2-10: Metal hand

Wood types do well with other wood types and with water types, as water gives nourishment to wood. Fire burns up wood, so woods should avoid the fiery element, lest the relationship consume them.

Wood types have to learn the difference between theory and reality, especially in the matter of relationships. They sometimes will have an ideal mate constructed in their mind and spend many years looking for this imaginary, perfect being. They also must overcome a tendency to just "get by" in a relationship, and learn to keep the connection alive and growing, rather than just hoping things will work out due to karma or destiny.

Metal Hand

The metal hand (figure 2-10) is square—square palm, square fingertips, and square fingernails. This hand looks a bit like the earth hand, but is wirier, with a hard, angular surface. When you shake hands with a metal type, the first thing you notice is the hardness of the palm. They have a steely grip, and you can see this determination reflected in their eyes.

Metal types have a great work ethic. If they have to choose between their personal needs and getting the job done, they'll pick the job every time. Strong-minded and a bit stubborn, metal types are hard to move from an opinion or attitude once they make up their mind. Usually, they are practical and realistic. This hand type is similar to the *practical* or *business hand* in Western palmistry.

Metal types almost always want to talk to me about work. In terms of relationships, many of them have learned that they prefer to be alone or in a relationship of convenience, with no strings attached. Like earth, metal tends to examine a potential partner from a practical point of view rather than taking a romantic or idealistic approach. Whatever emotions these people feel (and metal types definitely can have strong emotions) they refuse to show anyone until they trust them. In a relationship, metal will test you to see if you're a safe harbor to whom they can entrust their emotions.

On the job, the metal type is all business. Reliable, hardworking, and straightforward, the metal type is an ideal employee, a firm but fair supervisor, and a decisive executive. These people prefer to play by well-defined rules and like an orderly environment. Away from work, the metal type is friendly and personable, in a mildly detached way. They never forget a favor and will pay back a good deed with interest. Metal types like a balanced ledger. Independent thinkers, they rarely accept any new idea on trust alone. They must examine the new concept carefully and adapt it to their worldview. They get along well with others, although sometimes their strong opinions and honesty make it tough for them to have close friends.

Part of the metal's fear of intimacy is that their rigid exterior hides an inner core of insecurity. Metal types fear that if someone comes to know them too well, the other person will ferret out their weak spots and hurt them. They're like diamonds in that they're the hardest of all substances, but if you hit them from just the right angle, they'll shatter.

Metal types should find their mates among other metal types and among the free-flowing water types. The practical metal types generally do not get along well with the philosophical wood types. Metal tries to chop away at wood, dismissing the wood's speculations as impractical. Metal focuses on tangible reality, while wood explores possibilities. Metal also has problems with the intense fire type, as fire, if it's hot enough, can melt metal. The metal type resists melding his or her independence within the emotional cauldron of the fire. Air tends to irritate metal (just as air causes metal to rust), and this combination can be quite adversarial.

The romantic style of metal is direct, assertive, and businesslike. These people are uncomfortable with spontaneity. They do have a softer side (some metals, such as lead, are flexible and malleable), but it has to be teased out of hiding over time. Sexually, metal types are assertive and controlled. When they make love to you, they seem to be more observer than participant. The experience is satisfying, however, as metal types like to be skilled in everything they do. Over time, as they learn to trust within the relationship, they release their deep wellspring of sexual power and show their vulnerable side.

Now that we have an idea of what the elements can tell us about our personalities, let's take a minor detour into a related aspect of hand reading: the examination of hand *shapes*.

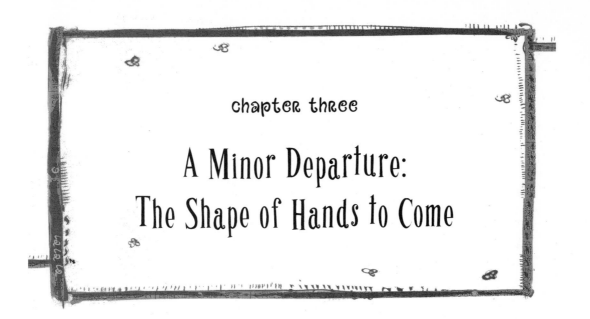

chapter three

A Minor Departure:
The Shape of Hands to Come

There is a very useful fact in palmistry that is so functional I would be remiss in overlooking it. Certain characteristics, combining elements, lines, finger types, and other factors, sometimes are found bundled together into archetypical shapes. The study of hand shapes is related to the theory of hand elements. Some hands combine certain features in a recognizable configuration, which can provide a very quick analysis of a potential companion's personality with very little effort.

Some schools of palmistry have more than three hundred hand types, but I've found that you can do quite well knowing about a half dozen of the more common types.

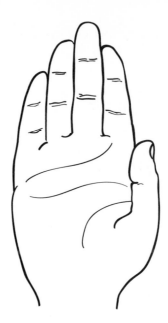

Figure 3-1: Conic hand

Conic Hand

This very beautiful almond-shaped hand (figure 3-1) represents a refined, sensitive, and empathetic person. A true conic hand should have a smooth curve, finely textured skin, and tapering fingertips. On a male, it indicates a sympathetic, sensitive, and intuitive outlook—not your average macho type. People with the conic hand seem to attract the personal confessions of other people, whether they want to or not. For this reason, I sometimes think of this as the "Dear Abby hand." Since conic hand types are sensitive to their environment, they are emotional barometers; they feel happy around happy people, sad around sad people, and anxious around negative people. Because of this sensitivity to the inner states of others, they tend to exercise caution concerning the people they allow into their intimate life.

The romantic style of the conic hand type is deeply caring and responsive. These people are in tune with their lover's every emotional quirk. You can pour out your heart to them and count on finding a sympathetic ear. Like most people with water hands (which the conic hand is a variant of), those with conic hands can become overburdened by the demands of the myriad needy people who are attracted to them as a moth is to a flame.

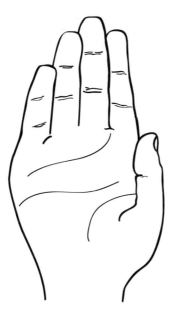

Figure 3-2: Spatulate hand

Spatulate Hand

The spatulate hand (figure 3-2) is easy to spot because the palm of the hand looks like a spatula: wider at one end than the other. True spatulate hands will have splayed fingertips as well. The spatulate person has a lot of internal energy and is always on the go. Air-type spatulates (those with a square palm and long fingers) tend to be a bit nervous, fantasy-prone, and at times unrealistic. They make great actors and actresses because they are extremely good at make-believe. I call them "shapeshifters," and they usually agree. Earth spatulates (square palm with short fingers) are energetic, amiable extroverts.

The romantic style of the spatulate type is energetic, spontaneous, and adaptable. Since these people love to run from one activity to the next, they can be hard to keep up with. They throw themselves passionately into one interest, but then leave it for a new, more exciting interest. Unfortunately, they tend to do this with relationships, so getting them to settle down can be a challenge. However, as spatulate people mature, they begin to wonder if all there is to life are fleeting, transient adventures and begin to look for something with more meaning. If they find an exciting, dynamic relationship, they can devote themselves to it with great enthusiasm.

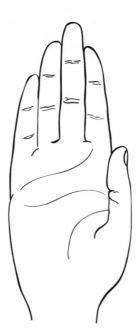

Figure 3-3: Psychic hand

Psychic Hand

The psychic hand (figure 3-3) is long and slender, with long, smooth fingers. The palm is narrow and often has many lines. Like the conic hand type, people with psychic hands have an uncanny ability to tune in to the emotional energy of those around them. They can spot when something is out of sync with a person and are so perceptive that they can almost read other people's minds. Their romantic style is deep, intuitive, and a little erratic, as these individuals tend to have mood swings depending on the emotional states of the people around them.

In a relationship, it's as though the psychic hand type can read your mind. These people can tell whether you're telling them the truth, so it's almost impossible to fool them or cheat on them. They always know what you're up to.

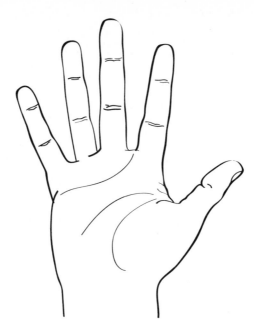

Figure 3-4: Realistic hand

Realistic Hand

The realistic hand (figure 3-4) has a square palm, square wrist, and square fingertips. The fingers can be a little knotty, with a large, firm thumb. People with realistic hands are down-to-earth and good with business, have a practical and realistic approach to life, and love order. They're honest and reliable, not very imaginative or dreamy, and are extremely self-disciplined. The romantic style of the realistic hand is open, businesslike, and direct. These people court their intended strategically, pointing out the logical advantages of the relationship.

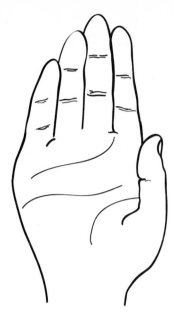

Figure 3-5: Diamond hand

Diamond Hand

The diamond hand (figure 3-5) is a variation of the spatulate hand, except the fingers taper inward toward the tips instead of spreading outward. It has a distinctive diamond shape that's hard to miss. Most people with diamond hands have a need for material security, and this definitely will play a role, whether consciously or unconsciously, in their romantic decision-making. Those with diamond hands are social creatures, loving to dance, mingle, and move about from party to party. Both male and female diamond hand types are conscious of their physical appearance and the impression they make on other people. Quite intelligent and refined in taste, those with diamond hands have an uncanny ability to determine whether something is the "real deal" or a shoddy imitation. Like all spatulates, they adore variety and novelty, enjoying good food, the latest styles, art, and literature. They have their finger on the pulse of the world and usually are up on current events. Diamond hand types have a flawless instinct for what is the best thing to do in almost every situation.

Romantically, those with diamond hands are flamboyant and demonstrative, and most often find that their most compatible partners are somewhat older than them. Unfortunately, like all spatulates, diamond hand types can be passionately in love with someone today and totally uninterested tomorrow. Therefore, it may be later in life than usual before these people decide it's time to settle down. This romantic playfulness tends to even out over time, and those with diamond hands enjoy a rich, exciting life with an appropriate partner. Since they tend to be picky, when they settle down it almost always works out in the long term.

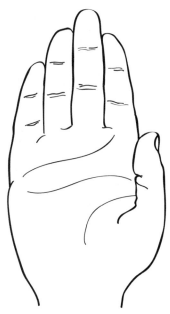

Figure 3-6: Action hand

Action Hand

The action hand (figure 3-6) as a square palm and short fingers. People with this hand type tend to be quick, impulsive, observant, and resourceful. They can dive into the middle of a situation and adapt as necessary as they go along. Their quick comprehension sometimes borders on the uncanny. Their instincts about people are instantaneous and almost always on target.

People with action hands have trouble explaining the logical reasons for their decisions, saying things like, "It just felt like the right thing to do at the time." It usually is, but sometimes other people see them as reckless and impulsive.

Romantically, people with action hands tend to go with their first impressions. If they're initially attracted to someone, they'll pursue it as far as they can take it. They like for relationships to move quickly and have trouble waiting for things to unfold at their own pace. Action hand types are used to making things happen in every aspect of their lives, and see no reason why romance shouldn't be the same. In bed, they're voracious lovers who arouse quickly and may have to be taught to slow down and touch all the bases.

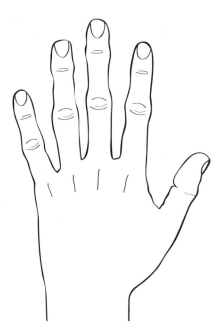

Figure 3-7: Philosophic hand

Philosophic Hand

The philosophic hand (figure 3-7) is a square hand with long, knobby fingers. Possessed of an unusually analytical mind, these people can really put things under the microscope. In an argument, they can tell you exactly what's wrong with you and what you need to do to fix it. They also can identify your good points and find nice qualities about you that you didn't realize you had. They're truly excellent at looking beneath the surface of things and figuring out how they work, people included. Their romantic style is a mixture of romanticism and philosophical realism. They love to explore alternate ways of thinking and to engage in new, unique activities.

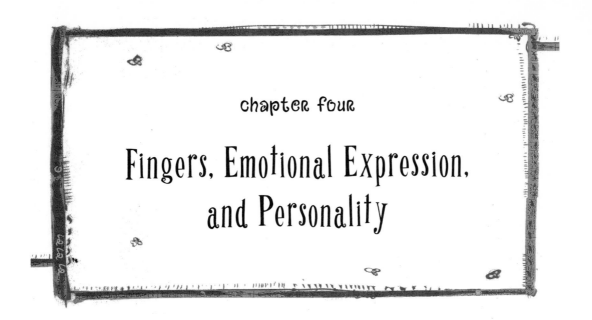

chapter four

Fingers, Emotional Expression, and Personality

Love is a truly mystical, miraculous, and wonderful phenomenon. To understand just how amazing it is, let's compare it to another important component of our existence: money. If I have a certain amount of money and I start giving it away, my supply of money soon will become depleted. If I'm too generous, I'll become bankrupt. Love, however, is inexhaustible. The more love you give away, the more you have. It's possible to love everyone you know—to love everyone in the world—with equal intensity but never diminish the stockpile of love you already possess. This is the magical quality of love; like the mythical Horn of Plenty, the more you pour out, the more you have remaining. However, love is like money in one respect: in order to give it away, you have to have it to begin with. And this is a serious matter. Many of us do not love ourselves at all. So when we try, no matter how earnestly, to love someone else, we feel drained and sapped. We're trying to draw water from a dry well.

Psychologists tell us that love is a learned response, which comes as a surprise to those of us who assumed love was something we're born with. If love is a learned response, then the fact is that many of us never received good quality teaching. If we're fortunate to have been born into a family with loving, generous parents, we should count our blessings.

But in this hectic modern world, it's more often the case that parents are too busy trying to make a living to teach their children the skillful practice of love. Most of us learn the lessons of love on our own.

The world can be a hard, critical place, and as we make our way through the trials and tribulations of relationships, we're bound to make a lot of mistakes. One grave error we make is thinking that love is the good feeling we get when we meet someone to whom we're attracted. If we learn about love from television, movies, and popular songs, then we imagine that love is what two people do in the bedroom with all their clothes off. Good feelings come and go, and then where are we? We find that sex is only a temporary euphoria, that an initial attraction can turn into boredom at the drop of a hat, and the person we thought was our soul mate turns out to be a pain in the neck. Like a drug addict looking for a fix, we roam from place to place desperately looking for true love, a love that lasts forever.

What we've overlooked in our wanderings is that we already have that love, glowing within our own heart like a candle in a dark cavern. All we have to do is release it, give it away, and allow it to cast its light onto the universe. It's only our own fears that keep our wellspring of love bottled up. We're afraid that if we show our inner light to others, they'll take advantage of us, hurt us, or make fun of us. Learning to love ourselves requires knowledge and insight. We have to extend to ourselves the same tolerance, forgiveness, and acceptance we're so willing to bestow on a beloved other. It sounds easy, but learning to love ourselves can be the hardest endeavor we'll ever undertake.

Love is an activity, not a feeling, and like all activities, the more we do it, the better we get. We can start right here, right this moment, by saying out loud, "May all creatures in the world be happy. May they all be at peace. I love you all, with every bit of my heart." If you can do this confidently and truthfully, even with that annoying loudmouth at work in the cubicle next to yours, then consider yourself skilled at love. The benefits are immense. The more skilled we become at the simple action of loving, the more love we'll attract to ourselves. This is a universal law, and there are no exceptions to it. Our instincts tell us that love is an essential component in our lives. If we can train our emotional expression to act in accordance with our instincts, then the world will become a much more loving place. Perhaps with enough love circulating around, people will lose interest in hurting each other.

We've seen how the element of our hands reveals our basic, instinctive personality. Our element can be seen as the foundation of a house. Our emotional expression, revealed through the fingers, is the framework and rafters.

It's no surprise that our fingers can reveal a lot about ourselves. After all, it's with our fingers that we communicate and manipulate. We write, draw, touch, wave, shake our fist, create, and destroy through the agency of our fingers. If, through injury or accident of birth, we cannot speak with our vocal apparatus, then we may learn eloquent communication through sign language. If the hand is the visible part of the brain, then our fingers are the brain's agents.

As a palmist, I place a great deal of importance on the information I find in a person's fingers. I probably read far more from the hand element and the fingers than I do from the lines of the palm itself, which surprises a lot of my clients. In fact, you can gather so much information from the thumb alone that you can base a full-length reading on it. I discussed Indian thumb reading in-depth in *Karmic Palmistry*, the second book in this series.

Our sex drive is not just a simple urge to procreate. Rather, it is a complicated mixture of various primordial energies, including aggression, pleasure, self-expression, and, in some cases, psychological traumas. There are many, many patterns of sexual behaviors, representing the complex spectrum of individual expression, and there's no way to list them all. However, we can generalize about several of the more common patterns that we experience and then go from there.

In the chapter on hand elements, we learned how to determine if a person's fingers are considered long or short. We also learned that a person with long, tapering fingers is sensitive to detail, somewhat picky, and has a streak of perfectionism. Short fingers indicate an ability to see the big picture, instinctive rather than logical reactions to a situation, and some impatience. This is good, but we can add finesse to this technique by examining each finger individually.

Forefinger: Jupiter

When considering the forefinger, the first thing I do is compare the forefinger to the third finger. I do this because it gives me a clue as to how to communicate with the person. A forefinger visibly longer than the third finger shows someone who is a natural

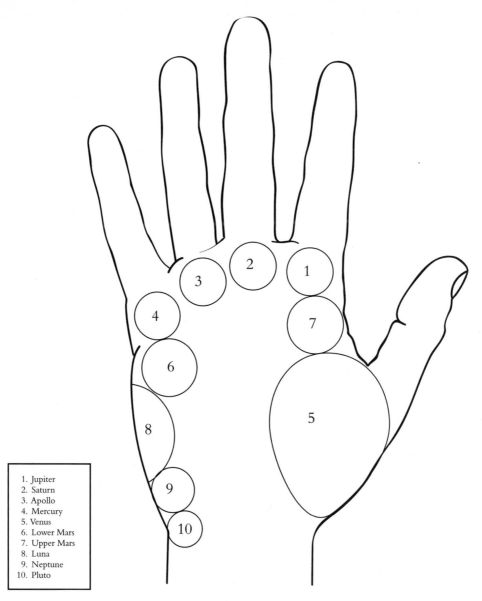

1. Jupiter
2. Saturn
3. Apollo
4. Mercury
5. Venus
6. Lower Mars
7. Upper Mars
8. Luna
9. Neptune
10. Pluto

Figure 4-1: Mounts of the hand

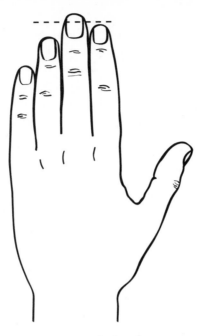

Figure 4-2: Long Jupiter finger

leader, who is assertive and prefers to be in control. If the mount at the base of the finger (figure 4-1) is large, then this holds especially true. The term used in classical palmistry for this trait is *Jupiterian*, after Jupiter, king of the Greco-Roman gods, whose every whim was law (figure 4-2).

True Jupiterians dislike being ordered around and told what they "should" do. When talking to them, you have to be diplomatic. As soon as you say, "You should do this" or "What you ought to do is this," they suddenly become deaf. In a relationship, they resist

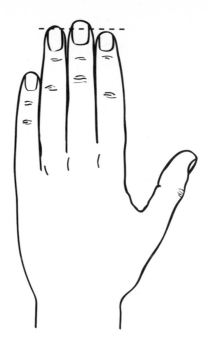

Figure 4–3: Short Jupiter finger

any attempt to control or dominate them. Total autonomy is their most cherished treasure. I usually phrase any advice I offer them as a suggestion, i.e., "You could *benefit greatly*
from listening to someone around you who knows you very well."

   If the forefinger is shorter than the third (figure 4–3), the person struggles with self-
esteem and may take things personally that were not intended to offend. These people are
constantly trying to prove themselves, not to others but to themselves. They're rarely satisfied with their position in life and are always trying to better themselves. In a relationship,
they tend to look to their partner for reassurance and inspiration. The tendency toward

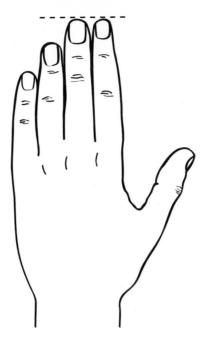

Figure 4-4: Napoleonic configuration

low self-esteem can manifest as a surface aggressive behavior, but the person's confidence is more fragile than it looks. You can topple these people with a well-chosen cutting remark, and they don't deal very well with rejection.

Individuals with a short forefinger usually give stunningly insightful and bold advice, but seldom take their own advice. They seem to lack confidence in their ability to apply their keen observations to their own situations.

There are subtleties even in this simple comparison of two fingers. If the first finger is longer by a nail's length, the person can be downright aggressive. These people get what they want through direct confrontation, with no beating around the bush. You always know exactly where you stand with them, because they will tell you directly. If the forefinger is so long that it's the same length as the second finger, it's known as the *Napoleonic configuration* (figure 4-4), and the person is powerful, aggressive, and competitive. These people almost always win, one way or another, in a battle of wills.

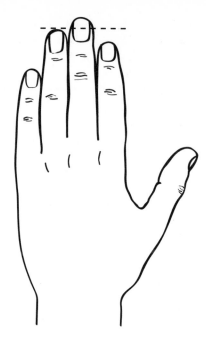

Figure 4-5: Long Apollo finger and Apollo mount

Third Finger: Apollo

If the third finger is longer than the first (figure 4-5), the person is *Apollonian*, named after Apollo, the Greco-Roman god of the arts, culture, literature, and diplomacy. These people are diplomatic and subtle, avoiding direct confrontation but obtaining what they want through more strategic means. If the third finger is wide as well as long, it gives the person a tremendous amount of energy when pursuing goals, especially in the arts, sciences, or sports. These people have lofty ideals and are motivated by working toward achieving their own personal best.

The mounts at the base of the fingers can show many aspects of the archetypal energies associated with a particular finger. I tend to think of them as showing what we enjoy doing. A well-developed Apollo mount shows satisfaction in the field of art, literature, fashion, or design. These people find their greatest enjoyment in creating things, designing, fixing, or remodeling homes, writing, painting, sculpting, or any other craft.

In a relationship, Apollonians tend to treasure harmony, even if it means sacrificing their own needs to prevent discord with their partner. They're usually pretty easygoing unless the self-sacrifice goes too far. For example, in a controlling relationship they can become passive-aggressive and sullen.

In 2004 a fascinating scientific study was carried out by Allison A. Bailey and Peter L. Hurd at University of Alberta in Canada,[1] which verified some of the theories of classical palmistry and also added a few wrinkles that most of us had overlooked. The study revealed that the forefinger/third finger ratio is sexually dimorphic; i.e., it exhibits a different set of manifestations in men than in women. They discovered that men exhibit the shorter first finger configuration much more often than women. This corresponds to my experience, although I used to attribute it to the different reasons for which men and women seek out the aid of a psychic. I had assumed that men with high self-esteem wouldn't be caught dead visiting a palm reader—it would be too "flaky" for them; but women, more in tune with their intuition, would be more likely to do so, especially if they had well-developed assertiveness.

Because of this dimorphic quality of the forefinger/third finger relationship, the authors call the Apollonian configuration the "Masculine Ratio." They found that it signifies increased competitiveness in sports and business, and sometimes manifests as aggressive behavior. Anger, however, was the same in both men and women. The Masculine Ratio also can indicate a lack of fluency in verbal expression, which is why men with short forefingers, no matter how assertive in competition, can appear a little shy in social interactions. You see this trait in many outstanding sports stars, who excel on the playing field and then shyly mumble their way through an interview. According to the authors, female observers see men with the Masculine Ratio as more masculine and dominant.

Classical palmistry maintains that a short first finger in men is a sign of low self-esteem, for which many men compensate with aggressive behavior and egotistical, pseudo-confident actions. Interestingly enough, the authors determined that this is not the case with women. The short forefinger in women ordinarily does not lead to aggressive and competitive behavior. The authors theorized that the Masculine Ratio occurs due to an abundance of testosterone in the womb. In women, according to this study, the Masculine

---

1 Allison A. Bailey and Peter L. Hurd, "Finger Length Ratio (2D:4D) Correlates with Physical Aggression in Men but Not in Women," *Biological Psychology* 68, no. 3 (March 2005): 215–222.

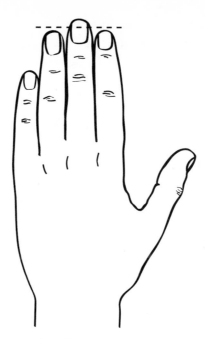

Figure 4-6: Balanced Jupiter and Apollo fingers

Ratio correlated with higher, more masculine scores on tests that analyze gender roles in society.

In hand analysis, we look for balance, so ideally the perfect configuration is when the first and third fingers are equal in length (figure 4-6). This person has an even temper, neither craves leadership nor is a blind follower (preferring to do his or her own thing), and possesses equanimity and emotional stability. These people can rise patiently and diligently to leadership positions in their chosen field, being careful not to tread on people on their way to success. In relationships they are flexible, tolerant, and willing to compromise without seeing it as a personal sacrifice. Their relationships build over time, as though crafted by a master sculptor, becoming richer over the years.

When Apollo curves toward Saturn (figure 4-7), the middle finger, it indicates that the person's creative expression lacks spontaneity. These people can be creative, but it's a more planned and structured creativity, like an architect systematically designing a house. Since relationships need structure, this is terrific, but since relationships also need some spontaneity, this can be a drawback as well.

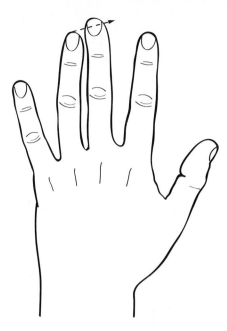

Figure 4-7: Apollo finger curved toward Saturn finger

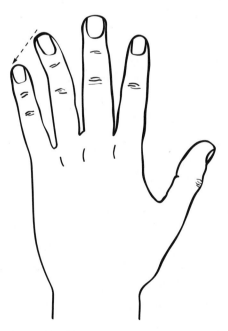

Figure 4-8: Apollo finger curved toward Mercury finger

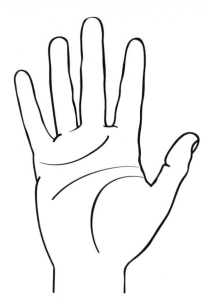

Figure 4-9: Ideal Saturn finger and Saturn mount

Finally, when Apollo curves toward Mercury (figure 4-8), the little finger, the person is talented in verbal creativity. These people make great storytellers and comedians. However, they might tend to exaggerate and embellish their description of factual events, so you have to take a good measure of what they say with a grain of salt. In relationships, they are charming and persuasive. However, no matter how much they may extol the glorious nature of romance, in reality they usually fall short of the grandiose promises they make. In other words, when in courting mode, they can promise you the moon, but once they have achieved their goal, these promises reveal themselves to be mostly moonshine. That's not to say that a relationship with them is built on dishonesty; just keep in mind their tendency to verbally exaggerate.

Second Finger: Saturn

The second finger expresses morality, ethics, character, and our sense of right and wrong. In other words, it's our spiritual finger.

Saturn is the axis of the hand, around which the other fingers pivot. Therefore, its importance cannot be underestimated. It's a difficult finger to read, but nonetheless is very significant. Just as the hand pivots around Saturn, so does the individual's personality pivot

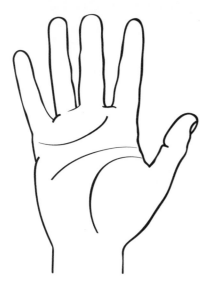
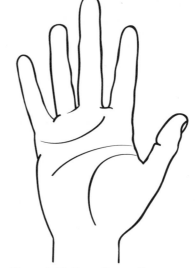

Figure 4-10: Short Saturn finger   Figure 4-11: Long Saturn finger

around his or her personal ethics. Saturn should be the longest finger of the hand, longer by at least a nail's length (figure 4-9). If Saturn is shorter than Apollo or Jupiter (figure 4-10), the person will lack a moral compass, following whatever trend comes along. These people seldom possess inner security or happiness; they are always searching for a spiritual belief or profession—something outside themselves—that will make them happy. As an interesting side note, I've observed that most severe alcoholics exhibit distortions of the Saturn finger: shortness, crookedness, or even outright deformities.

When Saturn is long (figure 4-11), the person has a good chance of finding inner peace and a strong spirituality that provides a solid rock upon which his or her entire character resides. Outside events do little to discourage these people; they possess an inner light that sees them through the difficult times. They know that everything—both the good and the bad—passes, so their equanimity is well-grounded. Their honesty is unimpeachable. In relationships, they open themselves completely, communicating directly and honestly.

Once again, we can learn a lot by examining the ratio of Saturn relative to other fingers. When the fingers are spread naturally, if there is a wide space between the second finger (Saturn) and first finger (Jupiter) (figure 4-12), it shows an individual who is unusually open-minded and tolerant of different people, lifestyles, cultures, and religions. If

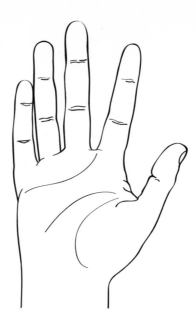

Figure 4-12: Wide space between Saturn and Jupiter fingers

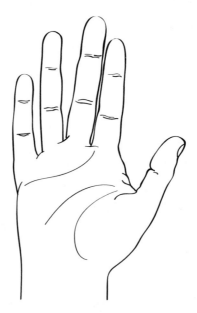

Figure 4-13: Saturn and Jupiter fingers close together

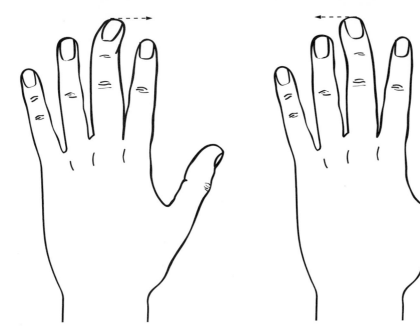

Figure 4-14: Saturn finger leaning toward   Figure 4-15: Saturn finger leaning toward
Jupiter finger   Apollo finger

Saturn and Jupiter are close together (figure 4-13), it means the person can be conservative and mentally inflexible; in other words, once these people make up their mind about a person or a belief, it's hard to get them to budge.

When Saturn leans toward Jupiter (figure 4-14), it's a sign that the person's morality is negotiable. In other words, if these people want something very much, they can suspend their ethics long enough to get it. Jupiter wants what it wants, and it wants it *now*, so when Jupiter influences Saturn, the individual's moral sense becomes subservient to the demands of his or her ego.

What about the middle finger that leans in toward the third (figure 4-15)? The third finger, Apollo, is idealistic, so people with this configuration have an ethical sense that is influenced by high ideals and the conviction that everything they do or create must express their spiritual beliefs. Apollo's influence sometimes gives birth to unrealistic expectations of their own and others' morality. In other words, they have high expectations about the innate goodness of others, and when the world and other people do not live up to these expectations, they can become extremely disappointed.

Psychologically speaking, in about 80 percent of the cases, Saturn curving toward Apollo can show a propensity toward depression and moodiness. After all, spiritual people tend to introspect constantly, and too much introspection, especially coupled with the high ideals that Apollo's influence brings, can make us only too aware of our own short-comings and defects of character. It's hard for people with this configuration to forgive themselves for being less than perfect.

As with all the fingers, the mount at the base of the finger shows how much of the person's energy is directed into the area the finger represents. It can provide a clue about what the person enjoys doing or how the person prefers to live his or her life. When the Saturn mount is large, the person has a practical philosophy and a live-and-let-live attitude, and is a wonderful teacher of abstract concepts. A flat mount (not a mount at all but a plateau) shows someone with an inflexible resolve who is self-disciplined, self-controlled, and tough as nails. These people believe that, with enough willpower and ef-fort, anything can be accomplished. Unfortunately, this makes them a bit unsympathetic toward people who do not possess iron-like resolve.

If there is a valley instead of a mount under Saturn, the person lacks willpower, direc-tion, and resolve. There is hope for these people, however, because if they become involved in self-help activities, they can turn their weaknesses into strengths. The concave mount makes them unusually receptive to suggestions and new ideas, so the trick is to make sure all suggestions and ideas are positive and constructive. As they develop stronger resolve and discipline, the Saturn mount will develop like a flat tire that has been patched and reinflated. I've seen it happen numerous times. Once these people become aware of their shortfalls, they do whatever it takes to compensate for them. Usually, the concave Saturn mount indicates that these individuals need help and support while they work toward self-reliance.

In relationships, a long and straight Saturn shows someone capable of long-term com-mitment, open-mindedness, acceptance, and tolerance. These people tend to remain faithful and committed. They are devoted lovers with strong philosophical ideals concerning rela-tionships, and are not afraid of crises or hard times.

People with a short Saturn have trouble sticking to commitments, so they tend to be-come discouraged the first time conflict arises in a relationship. They also seem to like life in the fast lane, so living with them can be a bit breathtaking. Therefore, the person with a short Saturn is more likely to be a relationship junkie, jumping from one relationship to the next. They also are less capable of long-term commitment, and are more likely to give in to temptation.

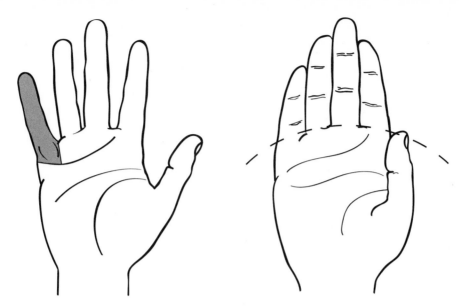

Figure 4-16: Mercury finger and
Mercury mount

Figure 4-17: Ideal curve of fingers

I realize that this sounds negative, but once again I want to point out that human beings are not robots programmed from birth toward an unchangeable destiny, but are possessed of free will and surprising adaptability. So even for those with a short Saturn finger, there is the possibility for growth and maturity. A strong Saturn mount can take the "curse" off of the short Saturn, showing people who have exerted themselves toward strengthening their resolve and moral stability. Sometimes they even go to the other extreme and become self-help aficionados, constantly going from one program to the next as they attempt to buttress their psychological weaknesses.

Little Finger: Mercury

Mercury, the Greco-Roman god of thieves, merchants, fortune-tellers, wanderers, sales-persons, and other parties who base their livelihood on adept use of their wits, was the son of Apollo and could talk his way into anything. So in classical palmistry we call the little finger *Mercury* (figure 4-16), because it expresses a person's communication skills, resourcefulness, and ability to charm, sway, and influence others. Through Mercury we

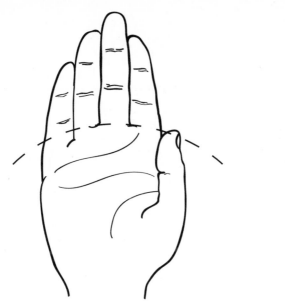 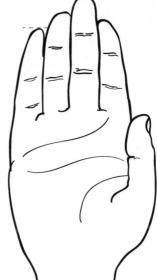

Figure 4-18: Low-set Mercury finger   Figure 4-19: Long Mercury finger

can determine how well a person communicates, if he or she can keep a secret, if the individual uses his or her words for good or twists them for personal gain, and how resourceful he or she is when the chips are down.

The bases of the four fingers should make a gentle curve (figure 4-17). If any one of the fingers dips down below this curve, it is considered low-set. A low-set Mercury (figure 4-18) can indicate poor self-esteem that manifests in self-deprecating speech (people who always put themselves down) and a desperate need for support and encouragement. However, due to the influence of Apollo, the person tends to blossom over time. A late bloomer, he or she comes into full actualization a bit later in life than someone with a normally set Mercury finger.

A well-developed Mercury mount reveals a born salesperson and communicator who loves to tell stories and jokes. He or she will be naturally gifted with a silver tongue. My aunt used to say that these people can sell you your own socks, and when you bend down to put them on, they'll steal your shoes and sell them back to you too. A low mount or a flat area under Mercury usually means that the person's communication skills are lacking. He or she may be a bit shy or uncommunicative.

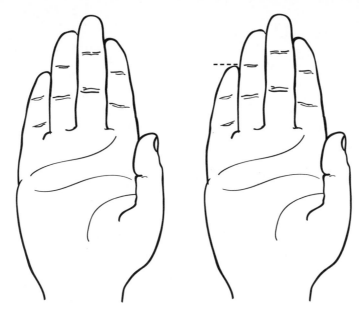

Figure 4-20: Short Mercury
finger

Figure 4-21: Honest
Mercury finger

A long Mercury, one that is at least even with the bottom edge of Apollo's fingernail (figure 4-19), belongs to people who have an infinite capacity for talk. Their oral self-expression knows no limits; they can talk to anybody about anything. They will be especially talented in marketing, able to sell buckets of ice cubes to Eskimos. Unfortunately, sometimes they don't know when to quit. Foot in mouth disease is frequently suffered. Romantically, these people have an endless supply of verbal ploys with which to ensnare their intended lover. They can be so charming and enchanting that few could work up the willpower to resist them. Therefore, don't believe everything they say. It pays to personally check any claims they make. It's not that they're dishonest, but sometimes their mouth runs away with them.

A short Mercury, one that falls beneath the first knuckle of Apollo (figure 4-20), indicates a person who chooses his or her words carefully. This person tends to modestly understate things—just as long Mercury overstates things—and is not given to boasting or self-glorification. Often mistaken for shyness, this personality trait actually reflects the desire of the person not to say anything unless it's constructive and useful. As my granny used to say, such a person chews his or her words carefully before spitting them out.

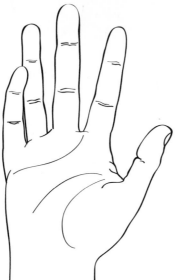
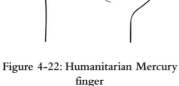
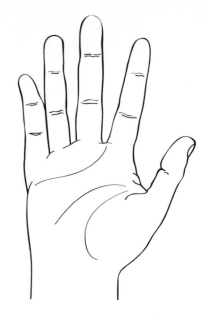

Figure 4-22: Humanitarian Mercury
finger

Figure 4-23: Mercury finger curving
away from Apollo finger

When the little finger is even with the first joint of Apollo, the person is honest to
a fault (figure 4-21). These people's observations are sharp, precise, and tactfully honest.
They're not big on flattery, but if you impress them, they'll truthfully and sincerely say
so. Consequently, if you fall short of their expectations, they'll candidly tell you that too.
Romantically, you always know exactly what you're getting and what they expect from
you in return.

When Mercury curves inward toward Apollo (figure 4-22), the person has a humanitarian instinct and loves to be helpful to others. Because of their concern for the welfare
of other people, these individuals refrain from malicious gossip, speak constructively, and
will keep a secret entrusted to them to the grave. In a relationship, they tend to be extremely responsive to the nonverbal communication of their partner, often knowing exactly what the partner needs before he or she does. Oddly, those with a curved Mercury
feel that they aren't worthy of the same consideration they give so abundantly to others.
I tend to correct them on this point; no one on the planet deserves any more compassion than anyone else, and that includes ourselves. Individuals with an inward-curving
Mercury find it hard to feel sympathetic about their own misfortunes.

What about when Mercury curves outward, away from Apollo (figure 4-23)? In many cases this indicates someone who's willing to stretch the truth to get a desired result. In salespeople, for example, they will say whatever they think will close the deal whether they believe it or not. They are skilled at debating either side of an issue (and even sometimes generating a third side), so trying to win an argument with them becomes a tangled trail of tangents and distractions. Few people have enough breadcrumbs to find their way back to the original point of the discussion when ensnared by one of crooked Mercury's rambling circumlocutions. Often, the other party quits in sheer frustration.

However frustrating their communication style, those with a crooked Mercury can be the life of the party when it suits them. They're possessed of infinite charm and a sharp wit. I think the circumlocutions and tendency to dissemble hide a sensitive and easily frightened inner core. Therefore, if these people learn to trust you, they will emerge from their verbal foxhole and show you their real self. If you like a challenging relationship, one in which you have to dig deep to find the heart of your lover, then this is the one for you. The reward is that you have something very few others have: you know who the person truly is, not the mask he or she shows the world.

Now let me tell you an interesting thing about the crooked Mercury. I know a lot of magicians (the theatrical kind, not the Aleister Crowley kind) whose job involves a tacitly agreed-upon deception between the magician and the audience. Most of the magicians I know have a crooked Mercury to a greater or lesser degree, demonstrating their ability to present to an audience a false frame of reference while actually performing something else altogether. In this case, and in the case of talented actors who also commonly have a crooked Mercury, their powers of deception are harnessed into a mutually agreed-upon theatrical diversion.

Don't mistake a crooked Mercury for one that angles out away from the hand (figure 4-24). The latter indicates a person who thrives on independence and chafes under too many restrictions. These people are slippery, so the more you try to control them, the harder it is to hold on to them.

Thumb: Athena, Rhea, and Venus

Just like the other four fingers, the thumb consists of three phalanges. But when we look at our thumbs, we're surprised to notice only two. Where is the third phalange hiding?

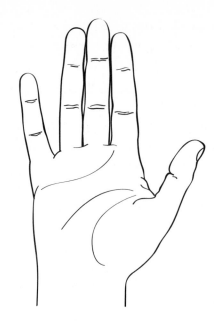

Figure 4–24: Independent Mercury finger

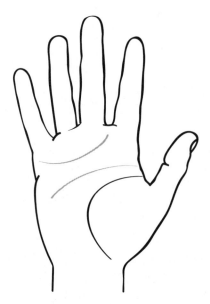

Figure 4–25: Venusian line (life line)

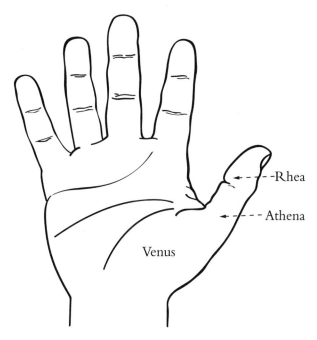

Figure 4-26: Venus, Rhea, and Athena

The third phalange is right there in full view, bisecting the palm of the hand. It's the part of the hand delineated by the *line of Venus*, often called the *life line* (figure 4-25). This broad, rounded phalange can take up as much as one-third or one-half of the total surface area of the palm. Because of its size, variety of anatomical detail, and importance to the hand, the third phalange is a rich field indeed for exploration.

As I mentioned earlier, the thumb of our hand is so rich with meaning that you can build an entire reading on this single digit alone. Without the thumb, the rest of the fingers are pretty much helpless. As the visible representation of our logic, willpower, and passion, the thumb truly is the master of the hand. Interestingly enough, the thumb is the only finger composed entirely of female goddess archetypes. While Jupiter, Saturn, Apollo, and Mercury were all males, Athena, Rhea, and Venus were females. Like the Norse goddesses (see *Runic Palmistry*), the Greco-Roman goddesses were every bit as powerful and dominant as their male counterparts. The thumb is also the only finger on which each phalange has its own archetypal designation. This precise and linear division of the hand into male and female archetypes is one of the many factors that brings the art of palmistry into dynamic balance.

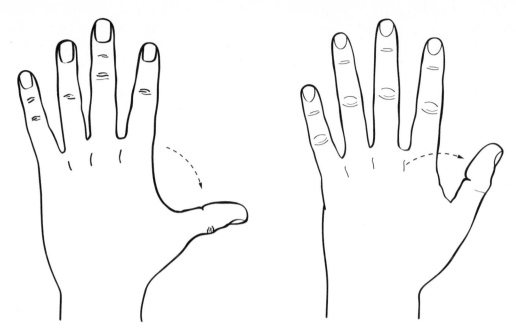

Figure 4-27: Thumb at ninety-degree angle   Figure 4-28: Thumb at narrow angle

For our purposes, Rhea represents willpower, Athena logic, and Venus—of course—passion (figure 4-26). First we'll look at the thumb as a unit before breaking it down into its three individual components.

Angle of the Thumb

A thumb that can be flexed to a ninety-degree angle or more (figure 4-27) shows an open-minded person who is tolerant of different people, ideas, activities, and points of view. Someone whose thumb bends back forty-five degrees or less (figure 4-28) will probably be more comfortable with people who think the same way he or she does, share the same values, and believe similar axioms. These people can be critical and judgmental toward people who do not share their views.

Sword Thumb

Press the tip of the thumb toward the wrist, and if it resists while still remaining flexible it's called a *sword thumb*. The sword thumb indicates someone who is hard to push around. They're not exactly stubborn, but they firmly resist attempts to control them. Like their thumb, you can push them only so far before they push back. Strongly self-reliant, they will be reluctant to admit defeat, ask for help, or give up without giving something their absolute best shot. Within a relationship, they are flexible, firm, and determined to make everything work out for the best.

Stiff Thumb

If you can't budge the thumb, or if the person resists attempts to push the thumb toward the wrist, it tells us that the person is stubborn. These people stand their ground and can be a little intimidating when going after something they want. This trait does not apply when the stiffness of the thumb is due to injury or arthritis; we have to look elsewhere to see if the person is stubborn or not. There are two classic tests for stubbornness: (1) if the thumb is inflexible, and (2) if the first joint of the thumb is longer than the second. If both of these qualities are present, it gives the person a double dose of stubbornness. In relationships, these people not only resist control but will rebel so strongly that they might actually do the opposite of whatever their partner tries to make them do.

Floppy Thumb

A floppy thumb, one giving little or no resistance when pushed toward the wrist, shows someone who is easy to push around. These people tend to lack courage and strength of will. They give in to pressure and avoid conflict, confrontation, and aggressive individuals. They often seem to lack vitality and energy. A seemingly paradoxical tendency is that floppy-thumbed people can be long-winded and opinionated about a subject they find interesting, often driving minor points into the ground. These people find strong emotion of any kind (pleasurable or negative) uncomfortable, so they will remain aloof and keep themselves detached from intense emotional involvement.

Tip of the Thumb: Rhea

Rhea was the Earth Goddess, representing deified Earth, the mother of us all. Rhea called upon her strong willpower to defy her husband, Saturn, when he was determined to slay their children. For the complete story of that primordial domestic squabble, you need to find a good book of Greco-Roman mythology. But here is an interesting thing: if you relax your hand so that the fingers and thumb touch, you'll find that Rhea naturally touches (opposes) Saturn.

We look at Rhea to determine the degree of willpower a person brings to his or her endeavors. We compare Rhea with her granddaughter *Athena* (the middle phalange,

Figure 4-29: Rhea longer than Athena

representing logic) to determine the relationship between the person's willpower and logic. If Rhea is longer than Athena (figure 4-29), then the person's willpower outweighs his or her logic. This gives the individual a tendency to act first, often aggressively, and think about the consequences of his or her actions later. However, this trait also contributes to the successful outcome of whatever he or she undertakes. These people simply do not give up. When they fall down, they get up, brush off the dust, and keep going.

The tip of Rhea represents how the energy of will is directed. If the tip of Rhea is square (figure 4-30), the person usually has good common sense and acts in a practical and rational manner. If conical (figure 4-31), he or she is perceptive, sensitive to detail, and

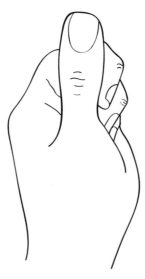

Figure 4-30: Square Rhea

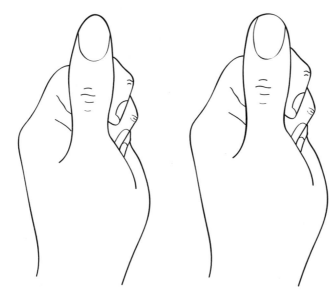

Figure 4-31: Conical Rhea   Figure 4-32: Round Rhea

impulsive. If the tip of Rhea is round (figure 4-32), the person is impatient with delays and has the ability to plow through obstacles and setbacks, accomplishing whatever needs to done.

A noticeably blunt thumb suggests strength of will and a tendency toward anger and aggression. These people must find acceptable outlets for their aggression. An overdeveloped Rhea can be recognized in a clubbed formation, which shows a tendency toward a simmering temper and resentment with the potential to explode into violent action over trivial causes (figure 4-33).

On the back of the hand almost directly behind Venus we find the *Earth mount* (figure 4-34). Although not literally a part of the thumb, it's so close that we'll pretend that it is. To determine the size of the Earth mount, ask the subject to hold his or her hand rigidly straight with the thumb pressed tightly against the side of the hand as though about

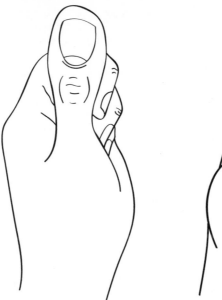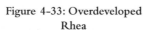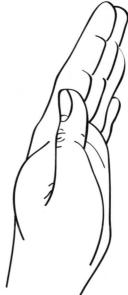

Figure 4-33: Overdeveloped
Rhea

Figure 4-34: Earth mount

to deliver a karate chop. The Earth mount will now be easier to read. When the Earth mount is large, the person has a strong attraction to nature. If small, he or she probably prefers the structured existence of city life. This person's idea of roughing it is a Holiday Inn without room service.

People with a large Earth mount are in love with nature. They worship the outdoors and have a greater appreciation than most for a good spring morning, a beautiful sunset, or the spray of water on their face at the beach. As an interesting side note, they also enjoy running around in the nude, so don't drop in on them unannounced or you may get an eyeful.

Figure 4-35: Athena longer than Rhea

Middle Phalange: Athena

In Greco-Roman mythology, Athena was the goddess of wisdom. She represents logic, rationality, and lessons learned from experience.

We've seen that, when Athena is shorter than Rhea, the person's willpower dominates his or her logic. When Athena is longer than Rhea (figure 4-35), the opposite is true: the person's logic dominates his or her willpower. These people tend to set goals that seem good on paper but take too much time and energy to bring to fruition. This means these individuals regularly bite off far more than they can chew. At the beginning of the day they may compile long lists of everything they wish to accomplish. But by day's end, many of the items remain uncompleted, which they find frustrating.

Sometimes those with a longer Athena may think too much before acting. In fact, they may think about a decision so much that they never make the decision. Relationships are scary endeavors, and people with this tendency can speculate endlessly about why they should not enter into one. They want to examine every aspect of a situation before turning in their final answer, and sometimes, if the decision is major, they would prefer to think about it forever rather than commit one way or the other. They prefer their actions to be safe and easily reversible, and they usually like to have an escape plan.

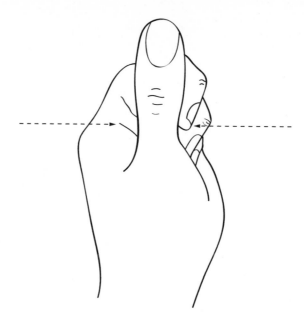

Figure 4-36: Diplomatic Rhea

Another trait to look for in Athena is a "wasp-waist," or hourglass, shape to the middle phalange (figure 4-36). This shows diplomacy and tact. If this spindle-shaped narrowing is found on the sword thumb or stiff thumb, it means that the person's stubbornness is tempered by discretion. If these people are commanded not to do a certain thing that they truly want to do, they will refrain from direct confrontation. Instead, they will smile, agree, and then do what they intended to do, when no one is looking.

Third Phalange: Venus

Venus was the Greco-Roman goddess of love, so it comes as no surprise that her area represents passion and overall physical vitality. This phalange is usually (and somewhat incorrectly) referred to as the *mount of Venus* due to its round shape (figure 4-37). The reason this is incorrect is because Venus is a phalange, not a mount, but who am I to fly in the face of tradition?

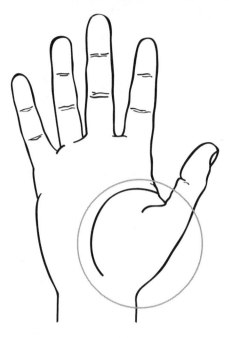

Figure 4-37: Mount of Venus

It's difficult to discuss the relevance of the Venus phalange without taking into consideration the Venusian line (or life line) that wraps around it and defines its boundaries. However, we'll examine the Venusian line later and devote our attention for the time being to the mount itself.

The first thing we look at is the relative size of the "mount." Is it flat, fully curved, or puffy like a pillow? A large, round mount of Venus, especially if it has a ruddy color, shows boundless passion, a strong, possibly insatiable sex drive, and abundant physical energy. People with a large mount of Venus usually have a great passion for music. A flat mount of Venus shows a deficiency of these energies. The person may lack passion, have little interest in sexual expression, and be low on physical energy. The mount of Venus can be affected by physical illness or exhaustion, so we shouldn't assume by a quick glance at Venus that a person has no interest in sex. A period of rest and recharging can puff the mount up quickly if the innate tendency for passion is there at all. Sometimes you can tell that the mount is deflated rather than being habitually flat. It has a sagging, empty

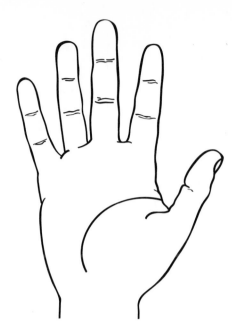

Figure 4–38: Large mount of Venus

look, like a deflated balloon. All it needs is a little pumping up (rest and recharging) and it will be fine.

If the mount of Venus is extremely large (figure 4-38), I caution these individuals about their sex drive, urging them not to allow their passion to override their common sense. There is a danger for people with a large Venus to become swept away by sexual excitement, so they have to watch out for this.

If a passionate lover is what you crave, look for a bulbous mount of Venus on a large, warm hand. This person not only will be an inexhaustible lover, but will be skilled in foreplay and erotic massage. When auditioning a potential lover, if he or she has a large mount of Venus, don't flirt with the person unless you mean business.

Horizontal lines spanning the length of Venus are called worry lines (figure 4-39), and a lot of them can indicate a nervous, fretful personality. Since these lines are on Venus, these worries are not about the owner of the hand, but about his or her family and friends.

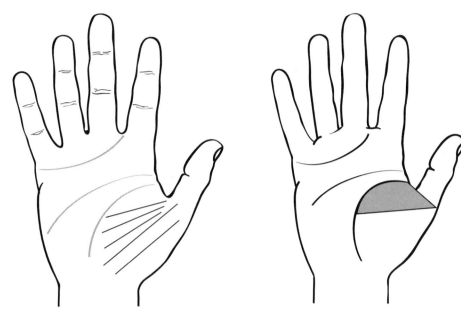

Figure 4-39: Worry lines   Figure 4-40: Area of family aggravation

Vulcan: The Area of Family Aggravation

The triangular area just above Venus is the *area of family aggravation* (figure 4-40). Lines in this area indicate stress caused by other people, usually those with whom we're emotionally involved, such as friends, family, and co-workers. When I mention to clients that I've noticed they have a lot of congestion in this area, they usually roll their eyes and laugh.

People with a lot of lines in the area of family aggravation have difficulty separating their own peace of mind from the emotional states of the people around them. They truly can benefit from developing objectivity, the ability to distance themselves from the emotional dramas surrounding them. On the plus side, they usually are very caring and protective, if a little obsessive, toward the people they care for.

Upper and Lower Mars Mounts

Most of the mounts of the hand are related to specific fingers, and so were discussed within the context of the Jupiter, Saturn, Apollo, Mercury, and Venus fingers. Although the Mars mounts are not related to the fingers, I felt it would be more consistent to discuss these

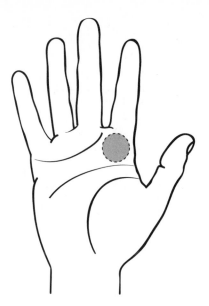

Figure 4-41: Upper Mars mount   Figure 4-42: Lower Mars mount

two remaining mounts in this chapter. The *upper Mars mount* (figure 4-41) is located beneath the mount of Jupiter, in between the head line and the heart line. The *lower Mars mount* (figure 4-42) is located beneath the mounts of Apollo and Mercury. In between these two areas is the *plain of Mars* (figure 4-43), which is located in the center of the palm just beneath the mount of Saturn.

Press on the Mars areas and check for firmness. The firmer the mounts and plain of Mars, the tougher the person is. A firm plain of Mars is a surefire indication of someone who is determined, strong-willed, and no pushover.

A weak or spongy plain of Mars shows weakness of character. The person can be easily controlled and dominated by a stronger personality. If both mounts of Mars are weak and spongy, the person can be easily swayed and dominated.

If the lower Mars mount is noticeably large, the person can be aggressive, combative when threatened, and eager for confrontation when challenged. When the lower Mars mount is large, the person isn't outwardly aggressive but will not tolerate attempts to dominate him or her. This trait often is found in law enforcement personnel and members of the armed forces. I've also seen it in skilled martial artists. If the lower Mars mount

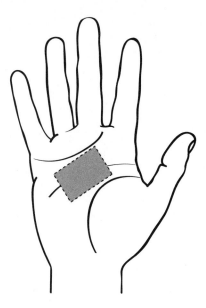

Figure 4-43: Plain of Mars

is too large, the person can be mulishly stubborn, even over issues that don't really matter. Compromise will be extremely difficult for this individual.

This finishes our discussion of the individual fingers. In the next section we'll zoom in even closer and take a look at the lines and other signs in the hand and how these relate to romantic and sexual behavior.

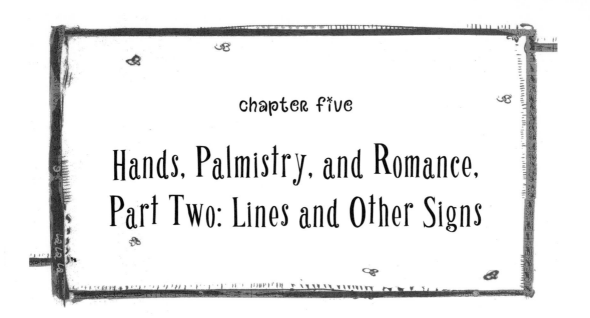

chapter five

Hands, Palmistry, and Romance, Part Two: Lines and Other Signs

The hand element is a terrific tool that gives us an overview of a person's character, the big picture as seen from a broad vantage point. Now we move in a little closer so we can examine our subject in more detail. The information we gather from the lines and other signs in the hand help us refine the Cheirological first impressions we deduced from the hand elements.

The lines of our hand reflect the impact of our minds, thoughts, feelings, and experiences on our personality (figure 5-1). Most of the lines found in the hand are formed in the womb during the second and third trimesters. For those who argue that the lines of the hand are simply wrinkles caused by flexing and moving the hands, keep in mind that the hands were formed before we were born, long before we became an artist, a scientist, a stone carver, or a housewife. The lines of the hand represent a fundamental connection to our brain. Everything we think, feel, and experience has an effect on these lines. If the elements give us clues about a person's instinctive reaction to life, the lines give us more refined information about the person's mental and emotional processes. Furthermore, the lines of the dominant hand give us an "update" on the development of the person since his or her birth. Experience changes us, and these changes are reflected in the lines of the dominant hand.

You don't even have to go into a deep analysis to learn a great deal from a brief look at someone's hands. A person with few lines in a simple pattern, without tangents, breaks, fraying, symbols, marks, and other interruptions, is a straightforward, direct person with a well-balanced emotional keel. A hand with lots of lines, especially if exhibiting tangled and complex patterns, can indicate someone who's a bit high-strung, sensitive, insecure in relationships, and emotionally needy.

Often, we see dormant qualities that we want to cultivate in a potential romantic partner. Perhaps we see a hidden generosity hiding beneath a self-serving outer appearance. If we're wondering if there's really something there or if we're giving in to wishful thinking, we can verify our hunches by studying the lines of the *subdominant* hand. If a trait is visible in the subdominant hand but not apparent in the dominant hand, then it is lying in a state of unrealized potentiality—a seed waiting to be cultivated into full bloom. When the trait is cultivated to full ripeness, it will appear in the dominant hand. Palmists call this phenomenon "bringing it across" or "crossing over."

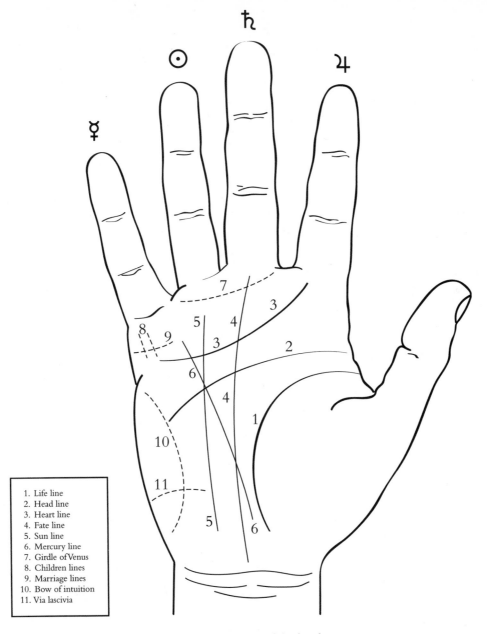

Figure 5-1: Lines of the hand

1. Life line
2. Head line
3. Heart line
4. Fate line
5. Sun line
6. Mercury line
7. Girdle of Venus
8. Children lines
9. Marriage lines
10. Bow of intuition
11. Via lascivia

Heart Line

A logical place to begin is with the area traditionally associated with emotional expression: the *heart line* (figure 5-2). The heart line begins at the heel of the hand, extends across the palm, and ends in the area under the first two fingers. Ideally, it should be smoothly curved and terminate exactly between the first two fingers, indicating a balance between giving and receiving love. Sometimes the line is long or short, and we'll examine the significance of this first.

Long Heart Line: Ending under First Finger

Those with a long heart line (figure 5-3) are strongly romantic people who put their lover on a pedestal. This line increases the risk of "falling in love with love." They can also be a bit self-absorbed, with dramatic emotional responses to relationship issues and a tendency to over-romanticize the relationship. Since the line ends near Jupiter, they like to feel in control of a relationship. Quite often they'll attempt to instruct everyone around them on how they should think and feel, and become resentful when others decline their well-meaning advice.

The influence of Jupiter gives these people self-confidence and the ability to look after themselves. When in balance, this gives them the capacity to clearly communicate their needs. In excess, it creates a person who thrives on the admiration of others. It's easy to enjoy a satisfying relationship with these individuals as long as you realize that their needs are very important to them. They like for their lover to see them as something very special and worth cherishing.

Balanced Heart Line: Ending between the First and Second Fingers

A perfect balance between giving and receiving affection, this line is ideal (figure 5-4). These people won't lose themselves in the relationship, yet will acknowledge the other's needs. They also usually express a great fondness for lovemaking. For these fortunate folks, a relationship begins with a strong foundation of mutual friendship, has an easy course of development, and builds over time to become a true partnership.

Short Heart Line: Ending under Second Finger

A short heart line indicates someone who displays his or her love in a strong physical sense (figure 5-5). Watch out! You may get your head hugged off. If the line goes up into

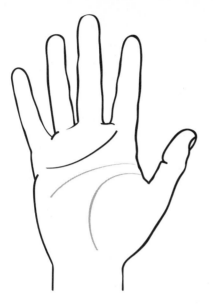

Figure 5-2: Heart line

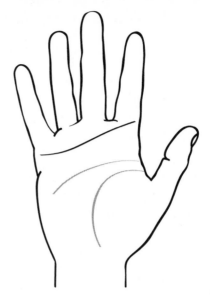

Figure 5-3: Long heart line

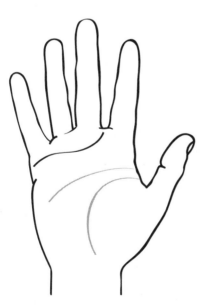

Figure 5-4: Balanced heart line

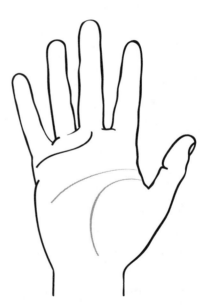

Figure 5-5: Short heart line

the second finger itself, it's called the *gift of mercy*, and shows someone who can sacrifice his or her needs for others. These people give and give and give, rarely thinking of themselves. It's difficult for them to ask for help even when needed, and it's equally difficult for them to refuse when asked to donate their time and energy to others. People with a heart line that terminates high up into the finger will give away their life in bits and pieces to others while never thinking of themselves.

The Curve: Up or Down?

Heart lines basically fall into two types: curved, or *physical heart line* (figure 5-6), and straight, or *mental heart line* (figure 5-7). Basically, a curved heart line represents feeling, while a straight heart line is more deeply cerebral.

Physical Heart Line

If the heart line expresses itself in a wide curve across the hand, it's called a *physical heart line* (figure 5-6). The person's feelings are very close to the surface; therefore, they break through easily and are expressed physically. In other words, a person with this line can't hide his or her emotions very successfully.

It's almost difficult for the person with a physical heart line to succeed at deception. When in a relationship with someone displaying this line, you learn that everything the person thinks or feels is communicated by his or her face.

The romantic style expressed by this line is, as could be expected, physical. Hugging, touching, and holding hands can be expected. Also, if the line is deeply curved, the person may fantasize and daydream much of the time.

People with a physical heart line also express sentimentality and idealism, so they could be especially susceptible to romantic seduction. Flowers, walks on the beach, and candlelit dinners complete with violin music playing in the background can win their heart without a struggle. Because of their devotion to the idea of romance, people with a physical heart line have to be careful not to "fall in love with love," which is a real danger, especially when the line is found on either the air or water hand. When I say to my curvy-lined clients that they've fallen in love a few times without really knowing the person and later came to regret it, they almost always agree. With people, just as with medicine, be sure to read the label first.

People with a curved heart line can be a bit fantasy prone and naïve, refusing to see the dark side of their beloved until it's too late. When initiating a new relationship, they

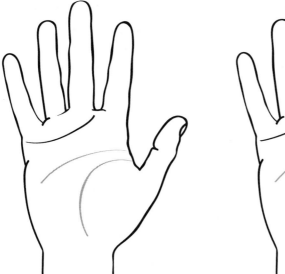
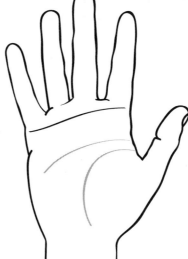

Figure 5-6: Physical heart line   Figure 5-7: Mental heart line

can become a victim of their own romantic notions, leaving themselves wide open to ma-nipulative people who easily take advantage of them. Swept away by the experience, they ignore the advice of friends—and even whatever alarm bells might be ringing in their head—until disaster hits. In retrospect, they always say they should have known better.

Mental Heart Line

The mental heart line is found on the hands of people who can hide their emotions (figure 5-7). No matter what they're thinking or feeling, their face and body give very little away. It isn't that they don't feel as deeply as those with a physical heart line—often, their feelings are even more intense—it's just that the feelings are buried deeper. It takes a while for their emotions to bubble to the surface. They consider it wise not to reveal too much of themselves to others and will tell you only what you need to know. Excellent at keeping secrets, these people always have an ace up their sleeve, secret knowledge they hoard until needed.

I suspect that these individuals have learned through experience that revealing too much about themselves can lead to hurt and emotional trauma. Therefore, close relationships are a little scary to them, and trust doesn't come automatically; they have to test you first. When forming friendships or romantic liaisons, they'll let you in a little at a time. It's as though they have a tiny valve inside, which they open just a bit, allow you to come a little closer, then turn it off.

People with long, straight heart lines can be possessive and a bit insecure, requiring constant proof of their partner's loyalty. They're extremely devoted, however, and remain with their beloved through thick and thin. They're attracted to the sexual and physical aspects of a person and are fond of physically attractive people. Straight heart line types are demanding lovers who require total emotional, physical, and sexual satisfaction.

There is a subtle clue that can be detected by those who know the mental heart line person well: the more chaotic and out of control their life is, the more they'll try to organize the external details of their life. Their appearance will be immaculate, their desk more organized, their house spotless, while inside they might be running around in circles, screaming.

In a related trait, people with a mental heart line express anger in a way that might fool people who don't know them into thinking they're quite calm. As their anger escalates, they'll become quieter and quieter, speaking in a cold, emotionless voice. When their voice becomes an icy whisper, it's a sign of rage. It's also a good time to find somewhere else to be until they cool down.

Some people, attracted to enigmatic individuals, see this type of person as a challenge. They enjoy peeling away the defenses layer by layer, like peeling an onion, discovering new treasures as they go. Is the reward satisfying? From what I hear, it usually is. The reason we take the trouble to crack a walnut is because we know it's worth the effort to get to the delicious kernel inside.

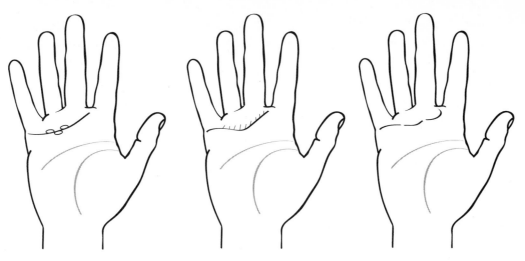

Figure 5-8: Islands
on the heart line

Figure 5-9: Flirty
heart line

Figure 5-10: Breaks
in the heart line

Islands on the Heart Line

Oval or round "islands" found on the heart line (figure 5-8) indicate periods of heart-break and disappointment. Each island represents a separate episode. A braided-chain configuration at the end of the heart line near the heel of the hand indicates an emotionally difficult childhood.

Sometimes there are a number of short lines shooting off from the heart line toward the fingers. These are called *lines of flirtation* (figure 5-9). People with these twigs like to experience a variety of lovers and tend to be a tease. They may never act on these urges, but they certainly think about it.

Breaks in the heart line (figure 5-10) can show periods of emotional isolation. These lonely periods may or may not be of the person's choosing, but are brought about by circumstances. Sometimes, however, the person chooses to spend some of these periods alone as he or she goes through a phase of introspection.

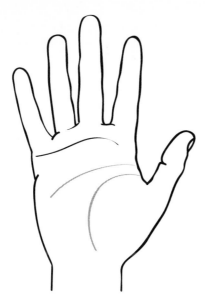

Figure 5-11: Practical heart line   Figure 5-12: "Safety valve" heart line

More on the Physical and Mental Heart Lines

The previous descriptions are for the two extremes that a heart line can take. In real life, the heart line might be somewhere in between straight and curved.

A straight line that tilts downward toward the head line (figure 5-11) belongs to individuals who are well-balanced between emotional expression and self-control; they can express feelings when appropriate but draw the curtain on their feelings when they need to. The straight mental component gives them more control over their emotional expression.

A curved line that straightens out near the end (figure 5-12) shows people who are essentially emotional but have a "safety valve" if they feel they've gone too far. When they're excited, you'll often see that they're about to say something, but then they close their mouth with a look of grim determination. Their safety valve kicked in, preventing them from expressing something they desperately wanted to say but would regret later.

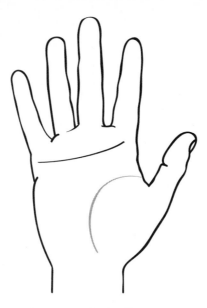

Figure 5-13: Simian line

Missing Heart Line, or Simian Line

Sometimes people will try to read their own palm from instructions in a book and discover that they have no heart line. They usually call me in a panic, thinking that they're deformed or that the missing line means they're condemned to lead a miserable life. Fortunately, neither of these scenarios is valid. In some people, the head line and heart line, rather than being separate, are fused together to form a single straight line across the palm of the hand. This is called the *Simian line* (figure 5-13). This is a rare condition, and the first time a budding palmist sees a Simian line, it can be startling.

To understand the dynamics of this line, imagine that the head and the heart run on two different circuits. When we're in a situation requiring an emotional response, the heart circuit kicks in. When a more cerebral response is required, the head takes over. This is the way it works for most people, although, if the head line and heart line are close together, the two lines tend to influence each other more strongly. For the person with the Simian line, there aren't two separate circuits. Both the head and heart run along the same circuit, so it's very difficult for these individuals to possess objectivity. When these people intellectually accept a person, ideology, or way of life, their emotions get involved. While they're experiencing emotions, their head keeps butting in, asking, "Why do I feel

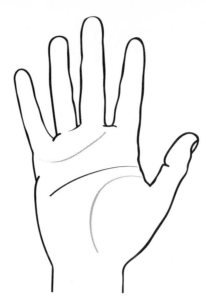

Figure 5-14: Head line

this way? And why do I feel the way I do about the way I feel?" This is because the Simian line is almost always straight, bringing some analytical aspect of the mental heart line into the emotional sphere.

Therefore, people with a Simian line are strongly passionate about their ideals, investing the energies of both heart and head in everything they do. They often become activists, campaigners, or sometimes champions of lost causes. When entering a job, activity, or relationship, both their heart and mind have to be satisfied. Otherwise, they suffer stress and unhappiness as their heart and head constantly argue.

Head Line

The head line (figure 5-14) is found just beneath the heart line. It begins on the thumb side of the hand, extends across the middle of the hand, and ends somewhere near the percussive (outer) edge of the hand. Head lines can be either curved or straight, and neither one is preferred over the other. It depends on what you're looking for in a relationship: logic and order or creativity and spontaneity.

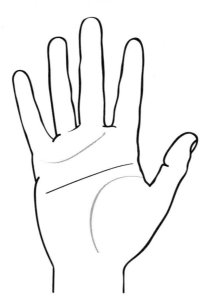

Figure 5-15: Logical head line

Mental Head Line: The Logical Thinker

If the head line is straight (figure 5-15), the person is a technical thinker. His or her mind tends to be orderly and logical. Such people are good with numbers and technical professions, but are not always great with people. They expect others to be as rational as they are, so they frequently become disappointed. They're also uncomfortable around people who act spontaneously and unpredictably.

Imagination and creativity aren't their strong points, but if a problem has a logical solution, these people will discover it. Excellent problem solvers, they usually see things in black-and-white terms. Once they make a decision, all gray areas disappear. They follow a logical thought to its conclusion and are hard to move once they've made up their mind. Sometimes they come across as know-it-alls, but in their case it's probably true.

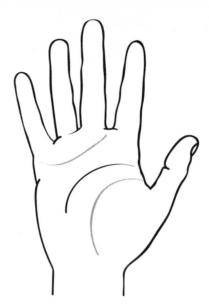

Figure 5-16: Creative head line

Physical Head Line: The Creative Feeler

People with a curved head line (figure 5-16) need mental stimulation in their jobs and relationships or they'll escape into daydreams and fantasies. A smooth curve shows a creative and original thinker. Too strong a curve makes the person a dreamer. These people will have excellent ideas, but these ideas most likely will remain in their head. These individuals need to learn practical ways of manifesting their ideas. Sometimes their goals and aspirations can be unrealistic, and they have to learn the practical skills necessary to plan and execute their ideas.

The danger of a strongly curved head line in terms of relationships is the tendency to idealize romance, sometimes to the point that these people avoid real, living, flesh-and-blood relationships in favor of fantasies that they generate in their head. They can live their romantic life vicariously through books, movies, and those Internet romances I mentioned in the first chapter.

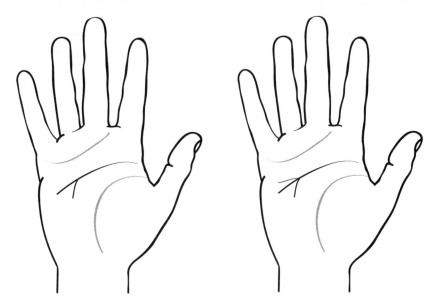

Figure 5-17: Forked head line   Figure 5-18: Trident

Forked Head Line: The "Lawyer's Fork"

The forked head line (figure 5-17) is an important sign for anyone who wants to create a product. A writer or painter must have both the creative inspiration to generate an idea and the technical skill to pull it off. For example, in order to write a book, you need creativity to have something worth saying, coupled with the knowledge of language to write well. A painter must know design, color theory, etc. People with a forked head line usually are masters of efficiency, figuring out easier and better ways to achieve a desired goal.

The forked head line is called a "lawyer's fork" because the person can see both sides of an issue, and argue eloquently for either side. In fact, if they want to, these people can argue one side of an issue and then switch sides mid-argument, without missing a beat. Their opponent winds up confused and frustrated. I've known people who like to do this for fun. Needless to say, these wily devils can be masters of manipulation, if it suits them.

On rare occasions, I've encountered a person with a *trident:* a triple fork (figure 5-18). These people bring a unique perspective to anything they do. I tell them, "Most people see things either one or two ways. You see things three ways—the right way, the wrong way, and YOUR way." They always agree. The third fork dips further into the part of the

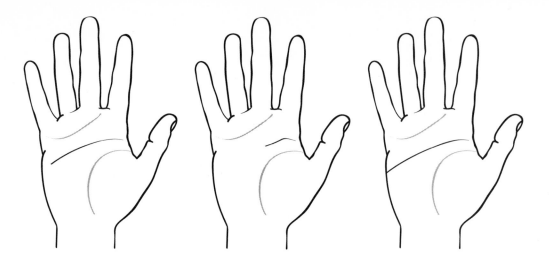

Figure 5-19: Long head line   Figure 5-20: Short head line   Figure 5-21: Very long
                                                                                head line

hand that represents the subconscious, allowing these people to add a special dream dimension to their world. They see possibilities where others would say none exist. They
have an off-the-wall sense of humor and often find laughter in situations in which other
people do not. A writer with a trident probably would create good fantasies or science
fiction.

Long Head Line

A long head line (figure 5-19) indicates a long attention span, while a short head line
(figure 5-20) indicates a shorter one. I find that the longer the head line, the deeper the
concentration. Individuals with a long head line who like to read will immerse themselves in a book for hours to the exclusion of anything going on around them. They can
absorb large amounts of information in a short amount of time. If a task requires laser-
like focus, they have it to spare. If the line is very long (figure 5-21), the person may be
a bit obsessive. In an argument these people can really bear down on a point and find it
hard to let go of a grudge.

People with a long head line like to collect reams of information before they make
up their mind. They also tend to stick with a bad job or unsatisfying relationship a lot

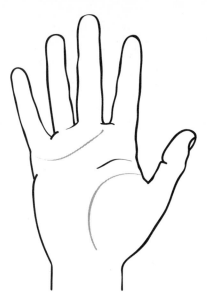

Figure 5-22: Short head line

longer than most people would. Their capacity for concentration makes them feel that if they hang in there long enough, things will have to get better. Sometimes they do, but sometimes they do not.

Short Head Line

People with a short head line (figure 5-22) usually have a shorter attention span, so when learning a new skill or absorbing large amounts of information, they do best with frequent rest breaks. Because of this trait, they may appear a little flighty, but don't make the common mistake of assuming that a short head line implies a lack of intelligence. Their attention span may be shorter, but they grasp the gist of an idea very quickly. They're also more spontaneous and adaptable to change than are those with an overly long head line. They like to jump into the middle of a situation, see what needs to be done, and formulate a solution as they go along. In relationships, they hate dragging their feet and would prefer that the relationship develop quickly.

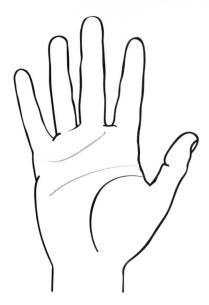

Figure 5-23: Venusian line (life line)

Venusian Line (Life Line)

Contrary to popular misconception and numerous Hollywood movie plots, the *life line* (figure 5-23) doesn't show how long a person will live. However, it's extremely useful in revealing quality of life; ability to weather stress, serious illness, and accidents; and how much positive energy is present. Since it also encircles the mount of Venus (the fleshy pad at the base of the thumb), it's sometimes called the *Venusian line* and can be useful in measuring a person's capacity for physical expression of love.

In the discussion of the thumb in the previous chapter, I mentioned that an analysis of the mount of Venus phalange is almost impossible without taking into consideration the Venusian line. We run into the same difficulty again here. The Venusian line defines the boundaries of the mount of Venus, and so the two are inseparable.

The Venusian line can be a good indicator of overall physical health. When the Venusian line travels close to the thumb (figure 5-24), the mount of Venus has a smaller reserve of energy. The person is always a bit tired and run down, requiring frequent rest breaks and tending to sleep a lot. It's necessary for people with a small mount of Venus to take

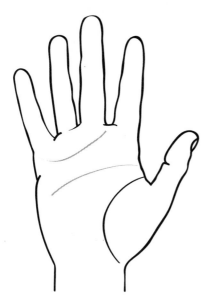

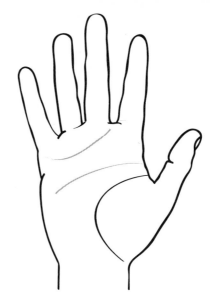

Figure 5-24: Close Venusian line   Figure 5-25: Wide Venusian line

especially good care of themselves and work on increasing their energy level. When the Venusian line spreads out well into the palm (figure 5-25), the person has almost limitless energy and the desire to stay active. These people love challenges and anything that gives them the opportunity to set ambitious goals, which they usually achieve. Their sex drive will be strong, as a wide, sweeping Venusian line is found only in those with a large mount of Venus phalange. When recovering from an illness or accident, their recovery time is short and the healing is complete.

Everyone has heard stories about people with a terminal illness holding on long past the death sentence the doctors gave them so they could live to see a happy family event, such as a wedding or the birth of a grandchild. According to insurance actuarial tables, death rates go down just before major holidays. I think this occurs because the hardier people, whom I'm sure sport magnificent Venusian lines, are holding off death until they can see friends and families one last time.

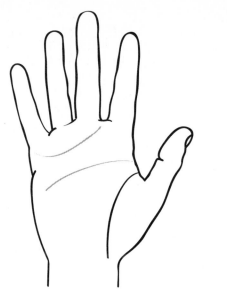
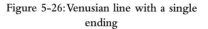
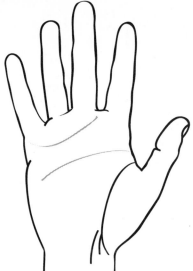

Figure 5-26: Venusian line with a single
ending

Figure 5-27: Venusian line with
multiple endings

An interesting area is the termination of the Venusian line, where it ends near the wrist. If it has a single ending (figure 5-26), the person is well rooted and enjoys stability and staying in one spot. However, if the line has two or more forks (figure 5-27), the person is a restless spirit, with a strong desire to travel.

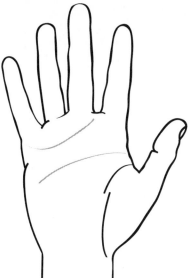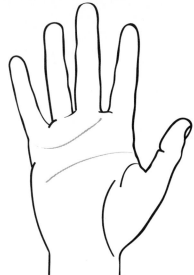

Figure 5-28: Inward break to the
Venusian line

Figure 5-29: Outward break to
the Venusian line

A Venusian line sometimes has a gap in it that breaks either inward toward the thumb (figure 5-28) or outward toward the heel of the hand (figure 5-29). These breaks show changes in the flow of the person's life path. If the Venusian line breaks inward, these people will become calmer and more conservative as they grow older. When they retire, they probably will enjoy a quiet life, preferring to stay at home, watch TV, or putter around in the garden. If the Venusian line breaks outward, these people will become more energetic, adventurous, and independent as they grow older. They often begin a second career late in life, sometimes starting their own businesses or going back to school. This is a good thing to look at in a potential lover. If you want to travel after retirement and your potential mate's Venusian line shows him or her sprouting roots as a couch potato when he or she is older, it's going to be a problem.

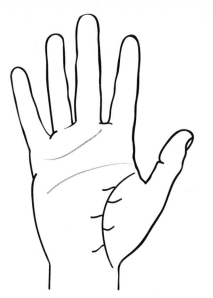
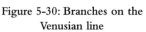
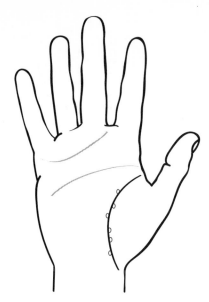

Figure 5-30: Branches on the
Venusian line

Figure 5-31: Potholes on the
Venusian line

Another feature palmists look for is the quality of the line. Is it firm, clear, and free of secondary lines branching out all over the place? Lots of branches shooting off the Venusian line (figure 5-30) indicates that the person scatters his or her energy all over the place. These people experience difficulty achieving the big goal because they waste their life energy on innumerable trivial matters. A lack of focus is the rule, and they have trouble separating trivial concerns from truly important ones, spending as much time and energy on minutiae as they do on imminent disasters. The ideal is a strong, clear line, free of tangles, breaks, and branches. It shows the ability to focus on goals and achieve them with diligent application of energy.

Sometimes you will notice oval or island-shaped areas on the Venusian line (figure 5-31). I call these "leaves" or sometimes "potholes," because they represent times in our lives when forward momentum—the expression of our life's energy—has become

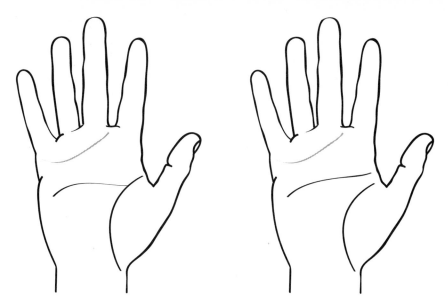

Figure 5-32: Venusian line/head line joined   Figure 5-33: Venusian line/head line gap

blocked through illness, accident, or traumatic life circumstances. If you stay with a frustrating situation too long and begin to feel like you may be stuck there forever, then you probably will develop a pothole on your Venusian line.

Some final information before we leave the Venusian line: If it joins with the head line (figure 5-32), it shows a cautious approach to life. The person will tend to plan carefully before making decisions and think carefully before speaking. If there is a noticeable gap between the Venusian line and the head line (figure 5-33), the person will be outspoken, adventurous, perhaps a bit rebellious, and not afraid of spontaneous action. Both of these personality types have attractive as well as problematical aspects. It all depends on what you want from your mate: security or adventure.

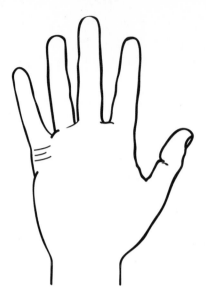

Figure 5-34: Marriage lines

Marriage Lines: Signs of Attachment

On the edge of the hand just beneath the little finger are horizontal lines known in classical palmistry as *marriage lines* (figure 5-34). In pre-twentieth-century palmistry, it was believed that these lines predicted the number of times a person would be married. This legend is so persistent that, even today, many palmists from the old school read them this way.

However, experience has shown that the predictive quality of these lines (at least as far as the number of marriages is concerned) is not as infallible as we would like. Because of changing times and a more relaxed moral atmosphere, modern palmists have redefined the marriage lines as *lines of commitment* or *relationship lines*, reading them to predict the number of emotionally important love affairs in a person's life. Unfortunately, it isn't exactly clear what factors separate an "emotionally important" love relationship from one that is less important. A fact that has long held true is that not all marriages are love matches; some are entered into for convenience, due to social pressures, or for other reasons that have nothing to do with the heart.

According to the eminent nineteenth-century hand reader Cheiro, only the clearly formed lines relate to marriage. Short lines relate to deep affection or a marital "near-miss"—a marriage contemplated but never entered into. Most palmists find that reading the marriage lines is a lot like predicting the weather: sometimes they are right on, and sometimes they're not even in the ballpark. People will have marriage lines from brief affairs, and I've seen people who were married several times with only one marriage line—or none. A friend of mine told me about a possessive mother who developed a marriage line over her adult son who lived at home with her. And what can the marriage lines indicate in polygamous societies, where the plural of "spouse" is "spice"?

In my opinion, it's obvious that marriage lines do not actually indicate how many times a person will be married. That these lines are connected to relationships is an observation that goes back hundreds of years, and it's a valid one, as we will see. But it doesn't make sense that a signpost as important as this could be dependent on ephemeral social factors such as changing sexual mores and the local definition of marriage. The problem of interpretation is based on a simple fact: marriage is a social convention, not a spiritual one, and as social conventions change, so must the interpretation of marriage lines. They have to be read within a modern cultural context, not according to some ancient book from another time and place.

The confusion surrounding marriage lines disappears when we understand that they do not necessarily indicate marital partners, but rather they denote *soul mates*, i.e., members of our soul family. Because these lines indicate a profound emotional commitment, I prefer to call them *lines of attachment*. If you have three lines of attachment, then you will meet three of your soul mates and have a satisfying, educational relationship with each of them. It may surprise you to hear that you can have more than one soul mate, but it's true—some people have hundreds. I discussed this topic in greater detail in *Karmic Palmistry*, the second book in this series.

The quality of the line of attachment is a reflection of the importance and intensity of the relationship. A long, thick line (figure 5-35) represents a relationship that lasts for years, culminating in valuable, life-changing lessons. Shorter lines (figure 5-36) usually indicate briefer, but no less important, relationships that teach us significant lessons about ourselves.

When the attachment line curves downward toward the heart line (figure 5-37), it means that you will enjoy a close, loving relationship but will probably outlive that particular partner. If you've ever had a dear friend, lover, or teacher who passed away after

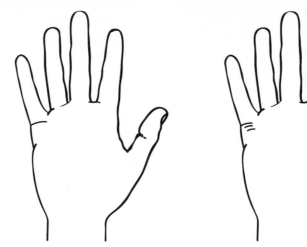

Figure 5-35: Long, thick
attachment line

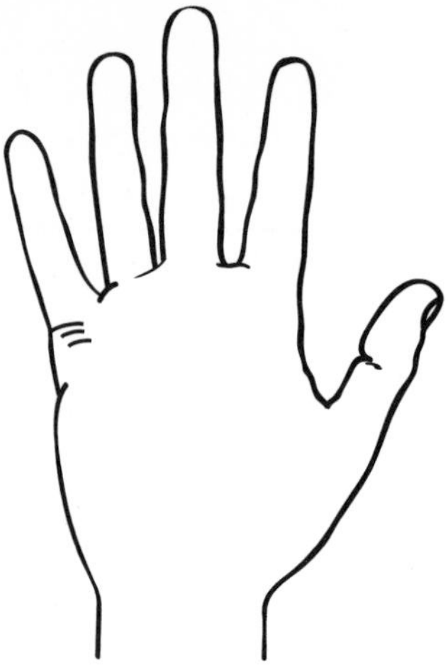

Figure 5-36: Short attachment
lines

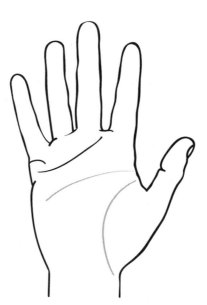

Figure 5-37: Attachment line curved toward heart line

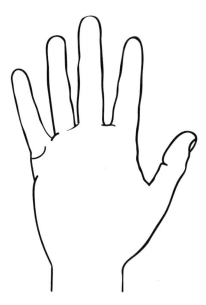

Figure 5-38: Attachment line curved toward little finger

helping you on your way, then you are familiar with this experience. Once the lesson is over and you have the tools you need to complete the work yourself, the teacher moves on. It's time to fly solo for a while.

When the line curves upward toward the little finger (figure 5-38), the relationship probably will be distinguished by arguing and conflicts of will. The lessons are revealed through debate and sparring. We've all seen married couples who constantly argue but can't seem to stay apart for any length of time, or friends who incessantly criticize each other's actions and decisions. Some families seem to be one step away from killing each other but flock together during times of crisis. If any of this sounds familiar, then you are probably aware of this concept. You can love someone without necessarily liking him or her.

You'll notice that many people have several lines of attachment while others have only one or none. Those with one line will probably meet and marry their soul mate, enjoying a close relationship until one or both of them pass away. Those with several attachment lines will enjoy many teachers throughout life and travel quite far on their spiritual and emotional journeys. The odds are very good that these people will marry one or more of their soul mates and have happy marriages.

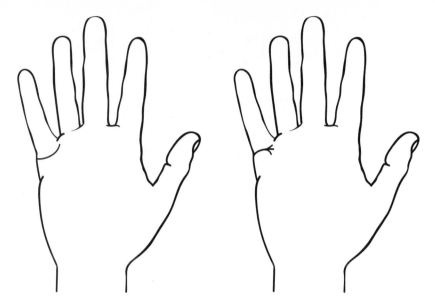

Figure 5-39: Long attachment line   **Figure 5-40: Forked attachment line**

Those with no attachment lines shouldn't worry. They still could meet their soul mates. The lack of attachment lines doesn't doom a person to a lifetime of solitude. These lines appear and disappear as we age. Sometimes a lack of lines of attachment means that the meeting of our perfect lover will come out of the blue, when we least expect it. Sometimes there are things we're just not meant to know.

Attachment lines not only predict good relationships, but also sometimes warn us that trouble is up ahead. All relationships have complications. We can predict the nature of these complications through certain signs.

A long attachment line, one that stretches past the confines of the area beneath the little finger (figure 5-39), denotes a close relationship with a lover made just for you. This is the common perception of the term "soul mate." The longer the line, the longer the relationship will last.

A three-pronged fork on an attachment line (figure 5-40) indicates that the person may be blessed with one lover too many. He or she must learn the pitfalls of the *ménage à trois*, for the middle line represents an intruding lover who must be dealt with. My grandmother used to call this configuration the "fickle fork," referring to the difficulty in staying faithful such a line predicts for the person sporting one.

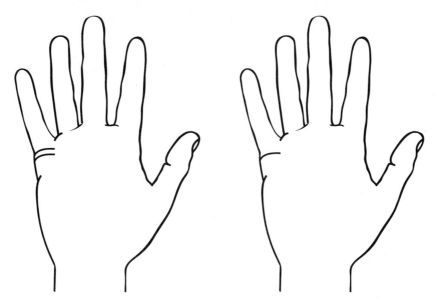

Figure 5-41: Two parallel attachment lines

Figure 5-42: Companion line

Two lines of attachment that run almost parallel (figure 5-41) indicate a businesslike relationship. The couple may stay together for years, but live emotionally separate lives. The relationship usually ends after the completion of a specific task. For example, they stay together until the children are raised and then go their separate ways. Usually, the separated partners will remain close friends.

A fine parallel line, called a *companion line* (figure 5-42, indicates a person who cannot find complete satisfaction in a marriage. To feel complete, he or she will need something else, such as a job, a beloved hobby, or, in some cases, an affair.

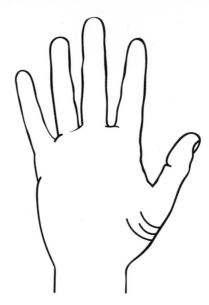

Figure 5-43: Adversity lines

I don't think this discussion of relationship-oriented lines would be complete without including *adversity lines*. These lines, which travel vertically from the heel of the hand toward the pad of the thumb (figure 5-43), indicate periods of conflict. Some Oriental schools of palmistry believe these lines indicate the number of enemies we attract to ourselves. I think this is true, in a fashion, but in Western society these opponents are not out to destroy us but are usually people who bring out the best in us through the dynamics of battle. This can be a business or romantic rival, a competitor in our chosen field, or a younger, more aggressive version of us. Being humans, we learn through struggle, and sometimes we need the competition of an opponent to force us out of our complacency. Rarely are these adversaries life-threatening, but they do keep us on our toes. Sometimes a line of adversity indicates a *situation*, such as a dead-end job, that forces us to reevaluate our direction, or a bad relationship that we stick with out of habit or fear. Forward progress is impeded until we learn to make an effort to escape the gravitational pull of the situation and move past it.

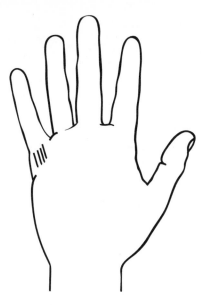

Figure 5-44: Children lines

Children Lines

Children lines (figure 5-44) are another source of trouble for hand readers. Traditionally, these lines are supposed to indicate the number of children the person will have. However, as with marriage lines, the children lines are sometimes right on and sometimes not even close. They appear to have been rendered obsolete with the passage of time and the greater degree of control we have over our procreation. With birth control, fertility treatments, and adoption, a person has almost total control over the number of children he or she will parent. Where, in this preplanned and orderly picture, can we find room for fate? Just as I feel about marriage lines, I can't believe that such an important feature of the hand could be invalidated by current practices, in this case the invention of birth-control technology. Therefore, I've come to the conclusion that the children lines are a way of measuring the person's capacity for parenthood. Having many children lines shows a need for just as many children, and having few lines shows that more than a few children would stretch the person's parenting capacity too thin. The lines can represent not only children that are physically parented but also adopted children, stepchildren, and sometimes even pets. If you want a large family, look for a mate with numerous children lines.

With this refined interpretation of the children lines, we see that they can be incredibly accurate. So pervasive is this parenting urge that we often see people practice it without knowing it. For example, we may feel an urge to take someone under our wing and mentor the individual through a difficult transition. This could be a younger person at work or young people we help through church, boys and girls clubs, or coaching activities. We become, in a sense, a surrogate parent to the person. Sometimes we also forge a bond with someone, a teacher or older friend, that is so strong we say the person is like a parent to us. These are just a couple examples of the countless ways in which subconscious influences, easily seen on the hand, can affect our behavior.

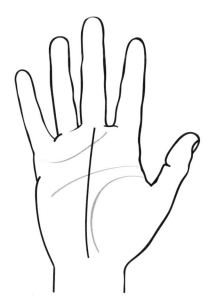

Figure 5-45: Saturn line (fate line)

Saturn Line (Fate Line)

In classical palmistry books, the *Saturn line* (figure 5-45) usually is called the *fate line,* in the belief that a person's fate is preordained and this line represents his or her inevitable future. Modern palmists have rejected this idea in the belief that a person's future is created, not predicted. The Saturn line shows the direction of a person's life and records the influences that determine the development of his or her personality. It shows the effects of environment, genetics, family, and personal choices on the psyche.

When I was much younger, I used to torment myself (especially in the violet hours between dusk and dawn when sleep refused to come) about the role that fate or destiny plays in our lives. Is fate blind, relentless, and preordained, like a computer program, to run its inevitable course, or is fate somehow aware and sentient? And if fate is aware and sentient, then is this sentience necessarily benign—or even sane? I finally decided that, in a practical sense, it doesn't really matter. We seem to have free will, and if there's some bigger plan, then perhaps we're better off not knowing it. Lord Buddha pointed out 2,600 years ago that so many factors go into our every action that only an omniscient being could determine what factors go into a single glint in a single eye in a single peacock's feather. Being the farthest thing possible from an omniscient being, I quit worrying about it. I think that fate and I worked out a mutual nonaggression pact: I don't bother fate, and fate doesn't bother me.

The Saturn line begins near the heel of the hand and reaches for the second finger. While it can begin anywhere in the palm of the hand, it must end in an area beneath the second finger. If it ends under the third finger, it's an Apollo line. If it ends under the little finger, it's a Mercury line. Both of these other lines will be discussed later on.

The Saturn line is one of the most changeable lines in the hand, often radically shifting in the course of a few weeks. To add to the confusion, some people have several Saturn lines, some have extremely short ones, and some have none at all. Because of the volatile nature of the Saturn line, it takes a little practice to identify it, but it's one of the most revealing details found in the hand. Any time spent learning about it is a worthy investment.

No Saturn Line at All?

In those charming Victorian-era palmistry books popular with the upper class during the nineteenth century, it was asserted that a person lacking a fate line was deficient in moral fiber and utterly doomed to a lifetime of failure. This is one of those persistent myths in palmistry, right up there with the one about how the life line predicts how long you will live. In my experience, people with no visible Saturn line are highly motivated, self-made people who create their own destiny. They usually scoff at the idea of fate, preferring to create their future with their own two hands. Therefore, success or failure is due entirely to their own efforts.

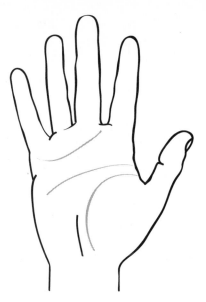

Figure 5-46: Short Saturn line
near the wrist

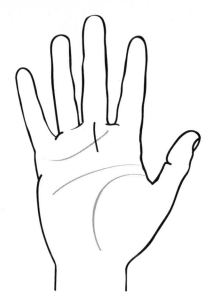

Figure 5-47: Short Saturn line
high in the hand

Short Saturn Line

The nature of a short Saturn line really depends on where the line is found in the hand. If the line is found nearer the wrist (figure 5-46), the person may be an early quitter who prefers play over work. When the Saturn line is short and begins high in the hand (figure 5-47), starting near the head line or heart line, it shows talents that ripen later in life. These people probably will try their hand at several occupations and interests before finding a comfortable place later in life. The advantage to this late arrival is that, when success finally comes, they're in a better position to enjoy it. You see this configuration in the hands of many people who return to school in their thirties and forties. Some-

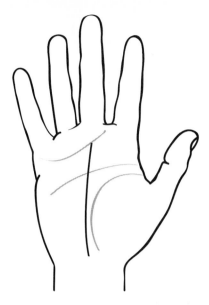

Figure 5-48: Saturn line ending before it reaches fingers

times the Saturn line ends before it reaches the fingers (figure 5-48). This can indicate a person who doesn't think about long-term security and is content to get by from day to day. Another meaning is that the person doesn't have to worry about his or her future because it's already taken care of. Maybe these people have money saved up or a good retirement plan. In some cases it can be a sign of great success early in life. The reasoning here is that these people accomplish their life's work while young and then get to play for the rest of their lives. This suggests that their future is open to many possibilities. Over time, the line may grow longer if the person's attitudes or circumstances change.

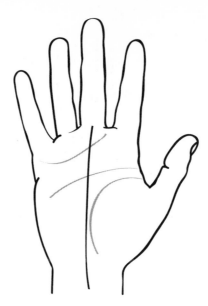

Figure 5-49: Long Saturn line

Long Saturn Line

A long Saturn line begins near the wrist and runs straight up the hand, ending under the middle finger (figure 5-49). This indicates an individual with a strong sense of self, who incorporates the traditions of the family with his or her own experiences. These people don't jump on bandwagons or follow trends, and they resist attempts to lead them in directions they feel are harmful or foolish. This is the "textbook" Saturn line you always see on palmistry charts.

Since the line begins near the wrist and continues in the same direction over time, this person will have had a clear sense of self at an early age. More often than not, these people bring their childhood goals to fruition in adulthood. Sometimes they follow in the family business, continuing the line from generation to generation. This configuration of the Saturn line can indicate a conservative personality.

The Many Origins of the Saturn Line

While the line of Saturn must end beneath the second finger, it can begin anywhere in the hand. The following are some examples.

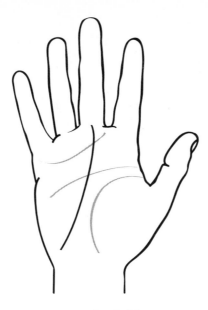

Figure 5-50: Saturn line in Neptune

Rebellious Saturn Line

When the Saturn line begins in the heel of the hand (figure 5-50), it indicates a person who tests established boundaries and prefers to march to a different drummer. Operating on a different mental level than those around them, these people sometimes feel "different" or out of place. Within the family unit, for example, they often feel as though they're from another planet altogether because their values and interests have little in common with those of the rest of the family. These feelings of isolation will plague them until they come to terms with the fact that they do see things from an entirely different perspective and that this is a wonderful gift.

This variation of the Saturn line begins in the part of the hand known as *Neptune*, representing the deep subconscious mind. (Neptune is the area of the hand under Luna, on the edge of the hand near the wrist.) This means that the personality is highly influenced by deeply mystical forces, of which the person may be unaware. Being motivated by a set of values different from that of most people has its advantages and disadvantages. The person with this quality is always the one who points out hypocrisy, asks embarrassing questions, and tests established norms of social behavior. These people are unique and interesting characters, willing to test boundaries and question authority.

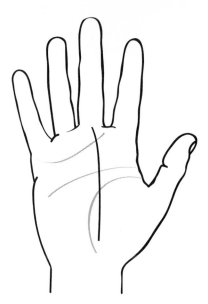

Figure 5-51: Saturn line in Venus

Conformist Saturn Line

When the Saturn line grows out of the Venusian line (figure 5-51), the person is concerned primarily with pleasing others. This is because the influence of family and society was very strong when this person was young, and he or she was pressured to conform to a certain standard of behavior. Usually, these people become more independent as they get older. This is especially true if the Saturn line swings away from Venus as it approaches the fingers.

You can see from these examples that the farther away the Saturn line drifts from the Venusian area, the weaker the influence from family and society becomes. Archetypally, Venus represents family and society, and Neptune represents our wilder, more primal and instinctive side. One reason the Saturn line is so changeable is that these two opposing influences are both immensely powerful. All our lives, we exist suspended between the security of conformity and the primal wildness of our mystical nature. These two opposing forces vie for control of our lives, and the effects of this dynamic process are recorded in the Saturn line.

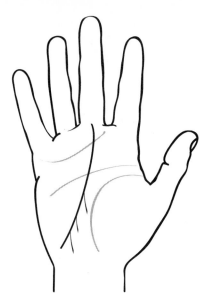

Figure 5-52: Saturn line with multiple beginnings

Multiple Beginnings

Sometimes there are two, three, or more beginnings to the Saturn line (figure 5-52), showing the many false starts the person will experience before he or she finally finds a satisfying life path. These people try on many hats before finding one that fits. Their teenage years will be spent exploring different identities, social groups, and interests. Usually they try their hand at several completely different careers before settling on one that satisfies them.

Each beginning shows a separate component of the individual's personality, shaped by the influence of family, society, and the person's own subconscious needs. All these myriad influences come together at some point in the individual's life, blending together in a wonderful alchemy that produces a rich existence and experience.

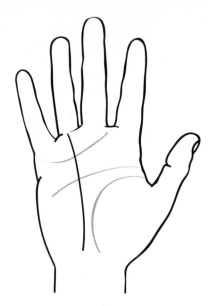

Figure 5-53: Apollo line (Sun line)

Apollo Line (Sun Line)

The *Apollo line* (figure 5-53) looks like the Saturn line except it ends under the third finger. The Apollo line is one of the lines that beginning palmists often mistake for the Saturn line (fate line). When present, the Apollo line is a good omen, as it predicts fame or success in a field related to fashion, entertainment, art, or culture—any activity that requires a highly visible profile. On the hand of a person aspiring to succeed in show business, it's a great sign. Most actors, actresses, and fashion models show the Apollo line, and I've seen it in the hands of talented musicians and successful artists.

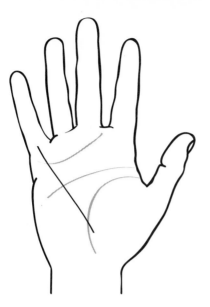

Figure 5-54: Mercury line   Figure 5-55: Nurse's lines

Mercury Line

Sometimes called the *line of communication* (figure 5-54), the Mercury line runs along the heel of the hand and ends under the little finger. When it's clear and unbroken, the person could earn a sizable income from his or her communication skills alone. It shows the gift of gab and enhances the person's charm, charisma, and persuasive ability. These people can wrap anyone around their little finger and can communicate clearly with an astonishing spectrum of people from all different backgrounds.

Nurse's Lines

Nurse's lines (figure 5-55) are located in the area of the hand between the heart line and the bases of the fingers. They appear as a series of vertical slashes that usually clump together in groups, like sheaves of wheat. When present, they indicate a person with sensitive, empathetic hands and a healing touch. These people will rub your back until you melt. They're also very good at soothing crying children, and animals love them for their skillful petting and ear scratching.

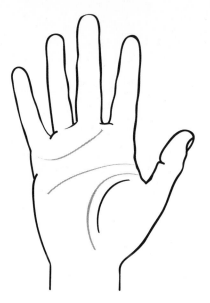

Figure 5-56: Line of protection   **Figure 5-57: Line of intuition**

Line of Protection

The *line of protection* (figure 5-56) indicates the presence of a spiritual guardian or protector, what some people call a guardian angel. This line looks like a second Venusian line. Some people have numerous lines of protection, providing so much security that they could be said to have a charmed life.

Line of Intuition

The *line of intuition* (figure 5-57) can be seen as an arc or bow on the heel of the hand. This special mark gives the person outstanding psychic and emotional sensitivity. These people are talented "people readers" and are profoundly intuitive and empathetic. Since this line encircles the area of the hand related to the Moon, these people most likely will also experience cyclic mood swings.

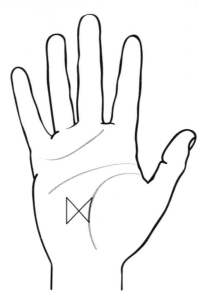

Figure 5-58: Butterfly

Butterfly

I love to find the sign of the *butterfly* (figure 5-58) on a person's palm. It shows a child-like spirit, free and playful, a wonderful friend to have around. These people just seem to attract good feelings to them all the time. The butterfly usually is found directly in the center of the palm, and the edge of one "wing" usually is connected to the life line or the fate line. When I did readings for entertainment at colleges, I noticed that most people who had a butterfly tattooed somewhere on their body had this sign on their hand.

Mystic Cross

One of the oldest classical signs of intuition and psychic ability, the *mystic cross* (figure 5-59) is found between the head line and the heart line. After all, intuition is the bridge between the head and the heart.

If the cross connects the heart line and the head line (figure 5-60), then the person will be exceptionally intuitive in both romantic and business affairs. However, if one of the legs of the cross is attached to head line but not the heart line (figure 5-61), the person will be

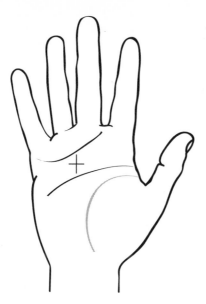

Figure 5-59: Mystic cross

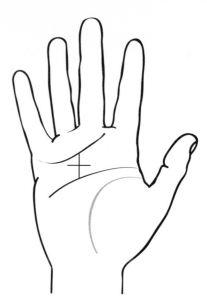

Figure 5-60: Mystic cross
connecting the head and heart lines

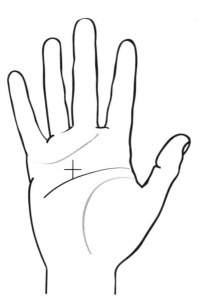

Figure 5-61: Mystic cross
attached to the head line

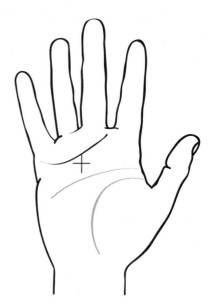

Figure 5-62: Mystic cross
attached to the heart line

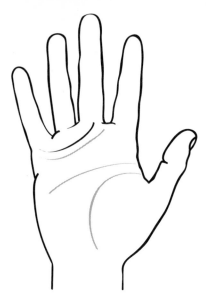

Figure 5-63: Girdle of Venus

able to read people in every aspect of his or her life except where the heart is concerned. If the cross is attached to the heart line but not the head line (figure 5-62), the person will be successful at human relationships but probably will have trouble making the correct intuitive decisions involving work or business.

Girdle of Venus

The girdle of Venus (figure 5-63) is like a secondary heart line, curving in the space between the heart line and the bases of the fingers. It's a sign of emotional sensitivity, empathy, and intuition. When found on a man's hand, he'll find that members of the opposite sex make better friends than other men, as he'll relate to women better than men. In a relationship, both men and women with this sign are almost painfully aware of the emotional cues of their partner.

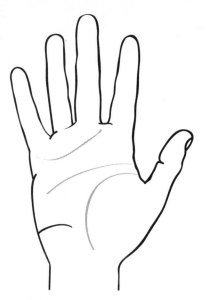

Figure 5-64: Via lascivia

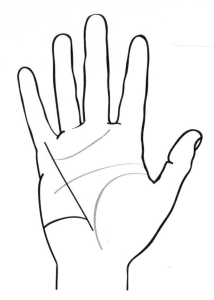

Figure 5-65: Via lascivia connected
to Mercury

Via Lascivia

A somewhat controversial relic from the early annals of palmistry lore, the via lascivia (figure 5-64) is associated with lust, drunkenness, debauchery, and sexual excess. It penetrates the mount of Luna near the percussive edge of the hand, reaching toward the mount of Venus.

Traditionally, the via lascivia is associated with excess sexual energy and an overdeveloped libido. According to ancient texts, if the via lascivia connects to the Mercury line (figure 5-65), the sexual urges are expressed openly and without repression. In other words, the person has a strong and readily expressed libido. However, if there is no controlling influence from the Mercury line, then the powerful sexual energies become blocked and repressed. Eventually the bottled energy breaks free and leads to hedonism, overindulgence in food, drugs, and alcohol, and outrageously promiscuous behavior. A strong, straight line is believed to belong to a person who freely enjoys expressing his or her sexuality, but if the line curves so deeply that it blocks off the entire area from the rest of the hand, then the sexual energy is deeply repressed.

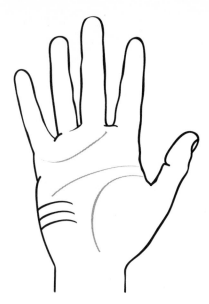

Figure 5-66: Travel or escape lines

The via lascivia has been linked to individuals who have allergic sensitivities and respond strongly to certain drugs, even prescription drugs. For this reason, it's sometimes known as the *poison line*.

Travel Lines: The Obsessive-Compulsive Personality

Travel lines (figure 5-66) are found wrapping around the edge of the hand and encroaching on the mount of Luna. In the past, these lines have been associated with a strong urge to travel. However, the urge is not to travel to some place in particular but to move away from the current situation. In a sense, it's a subconscious urge to escape an untenable reality. Hence, the person may find his or her escape through addictive or obsessive-compulsive behavior. Many people I've counseled with a family history of addiction have these lines, and I caution them about the perils of indulging in addictive behaviors.

Addiction takes many forms. Alcohol, food, drugs, and sex are the most common manifestations, but work, relationships, conspiracy theories—pretty much anything—can become the focus of the obsessive-compulsive behavior.

Having an obsessive component to your personality may not always be a bad thing. After all, if you're having brain surgery, you hope with all your heart that your doctor is obsessed with your brain and that his or her thoughts aren't wandering off to the golf course or the attractive anesthesiologist. However, if we find within ourselves the tendency toward obsessive behavior, we can choose to apply it constructively: like that brain surgeon, we can direct it into useful and productive channels rather than succumbing to self-destructive yearnings.

There are literally hundreds more lines and signs we can find in different hands, but a complete listing and description of them would take several large volumes, and I guarantee that we would still miss quite a few. In spite of that, I hope this chapter gives you a good understanding of the more common characteristics that can be read from the lines on the hand.

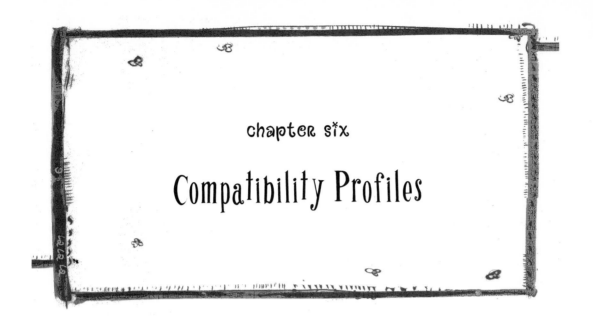

chapter six

Compatibility Profiles

I think that love, more than any other emotion, is filtered through the network of mental circuitry comprising the sum total of who we are: our psychological "profile." If we're insecure, angry, resentful, or biased, this shows in the manner in which we express love. If we're happy, free, open-minded, and courageous, we tend to express our love through these filters. Philosophers, religious leaders, and, more recently, psychologists have told us that we realize only the barest fraction of our full potential. If we could actualize the full power of our free and loving hearts, who knows what miracles we could accomplish?

When two people come together to share a mutual experience of love, we find a very complicated situation developing. The emotional currents have to filter through not one, but two, sets of mental circuitry, perhaps two sets that are completely different and far removed from each other. Communication is all but impossible unless both partners speak the same language. Is it any wonder that even when we're together with other people, we nevertheless often feel quite isolated and alone?

When we enter into a relationship, we're treading upon new and unfamiliar terrain. It helps immensely if we commence the voyage with a reliable map. To this end, I've constructed a series of compatibility profiles based on the elements to help predict typical relationship dynamics that arise in different combinations of couples. As you read these compatibility sketches, bear in mind that the profiles use each element in its purest form, and that very few people in real life fall entirely into a pure elemental classification. But since most people are predominately one element or another, this is a good starting point. We can improve our knowledge as we go along.

Let's take another look at the rules governing the elements:

Wood conquers earth

Earth conquers water

Water conquers fire

Fire conquers metal

Metal conquers wood (think of an ax felling a tree)

Air conquers all

Therefore:

- Earth and fire are complementary

- Earth and water are complementary

- Fire and air are complementary

- Earth and air are antagonistic

- Water and air are antagonistic

- Fire and water are antagonistic

And among the rarer elements:

- Metal and water are complementary

- Metal and earth are complementary

- Metal and air are antagonistic

- Metal and fire are antagonistic

- Wood and water are complementary

- Wood and earth are complementary

- Wood and air are complementary

- Wood and fire are antagonistic

- Wood and metal are antagonistic

- Metal and fire are antagonistic

Everything is relative, even relationships. I recall one relationship I had with a fire type, in which she thought I was boring. But in another relationship with an earth type, I was unpredictable and wild. Which was I? Either? Both? Neither? Nobody exists in a static, isolated state. We tend to define ourselves through comparison to other people. Whether you're stable, unpredictable, easily aroused, or patient depends on who you're with at the time. How we see ourselves may be at total odds with how other people see us. We tend to interpret reality through our own filters.

The style of palm reading that evolved from the principles of the elements has certain rules concerning the interactions of the various elements. As we examine these principles, bear in mind that these "rules" are guidelines, not universal laws. However, through the comparison of the elements we observe the predictable patterns that appear in different permutations of the elements in relationships.

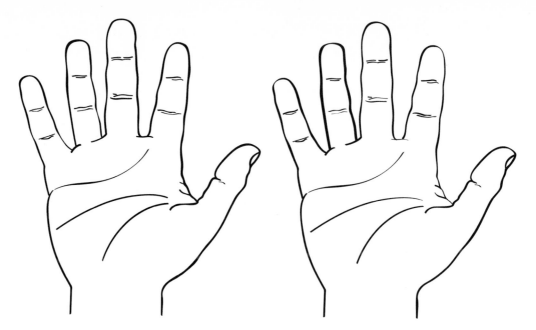

Figure 6-1: Earth hand/earth hand

Earth/Earth

There's a persistent romantic myth that says, in essence, "opposites attract." This is based on the intrigue we experience when introduced to a novel, exotic situation or person. Unfortunately, while opposites initially may find each other fascinating, we tend to find our best life mates among people who share our basic principles. Of course, there are exceptions to this rule, but generally speaking it's just easier to get along with people who are most like us. There are fewer areas of opportunity for conflict. There's also, consequently, less opportunity for change and growth in the relationship. It's a trade-off. Humans are programmed to respond to a conflict by adapting to stressful conditions and conquering them. Some conflict and friction may be useful in encouraging awareness of a different point of view, but only if each partner resolves not to take the disagreement personally.

The earth/earth relationship (figure 6-1) probably started out with a mutual investigation into each other's viewpoints and qualities. Remember, earth approaches a relationship in a practical manner, making sure the person under consideration will be a reliable and secure partner. Earth loves security, stability, and a predictable series of life transitions; therefore, both of these partners are terrific planners, working together to achieve similar goals. An earth/earth mating may seem to lack spontaneity and passion, but this is one of the more comfortable and contented elemental pairings. Both partners are on the same page in terms of children, family values, and finances. Both will place great importance on the relationship itself, being willing to set aside their individual needs for the good of the family unit.

One of the potential areas to work on is the tendency of earth types to become too focused on responsibilities and work to the detriment of their playful qualities. Sometimes they have to make an effort to break out of that work mode and play a little.

Sexually, earth is a devoted and constant lover, if somewhat predictable. Sexual expression tends to fall into regular patterns, even occurring on a schedule (Wednesdays and Saturdays, for example). Before earth will experiment with more exotic lovemaking styles, he or she likes to feel secure and safe. Once the door is closed, the sky can be the limit, but nothing throws an earth type off his or her tracks like the door suddenly opening and the kids rushing in.

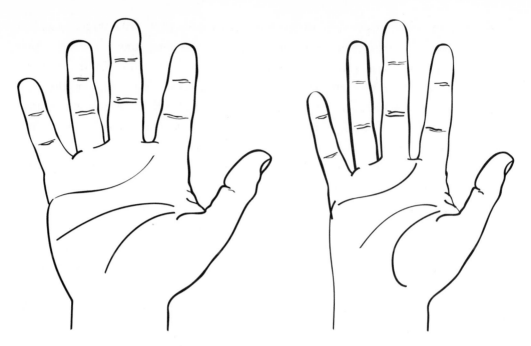

Figure 6-2: Earth hand/air hand

Earth/Air

Earth and air (figure 6-2) are antagonistic elements. Earth approaches problems in a rational and practical manner, while air relies more on intuition and emotions. Air is intuitive, receptive, and subtle, while earth is more verbal and direct. For an air, a situation has to feel right before he or she will accept it wholeheartedly. Earth may sometimes try to force air to logically discuss an issue, while air prefers expressing his or her feelings. Think of it this way: earth's communication style is more factual, like a reporter, while air's is more literary, like that of a poet. Both partners must remember that both ways of understanding the world are valid. At times, earth finds air hard to fathom and even given to fantasy-prone thinking, while air wishes that earth would relax and be more spontaneous. Earth also has a joking sense of humor, and may accidentally hurt air's feelings without realizing it.

In a debate, earth doesn't stand a chance against air. Air's quick, facile mind is always two steps ahead of the linear-thinking earth. Air can generate tangents, weave a conceptual web that earth cannot hope to penetrate, and even argue both sides of an issue, switching in mid-argument, if it so suits him or her. Earth quite often has no recourse but to withdraw from the battle, sullen and resentful.

If you think about how strong gales of wind can wreak havoc on the Earth, uprooting foliage and devastating the landscape, then you can get an idea of how the well-grounded earth person fears the disruptive influence of the air person. On the other hand, a strong air will subconsciously attempt to stir up the earth's steadfast attitudes and lifestyle, "unrooting" earth. Earth often has an objective, detached way of looking at relationship problems, seeking rational solutions, while air, being intuitive and sensitive, seeks emotional balance. If both partners recognize this elemental struggle, then each can give the other more latitude for individual self-expression without taking personally the deviations from the norm. This conflict cannot be ignored. It can escalate over time to the point of wiping away all the good points of the relationship, leaving rubble in its wake. Properly tamed, however, it can lead to an energetic and dynamic (if at times confusing) life together.

Earth makes a terrific parent, often calling upon his or her inner childlike nature to be as much a playmate as a parent. These people encourage their children to take on practical, secure, money-making professions, while air parents, who are idealistically high-minded, imagine their children becoming great poets, scholars, artists, or scientists. Between earth's practicality and air's idealism, the children have a rich variety of points of view to draw upon when determining their life's path.

There can be some conflict in terms of money. Earth believes in security, saving money for a rainy day. To an air, money is just a means to an end. If air types have money, they can think of all kinds of interesting ways to spend it. Over time, earth can learn to relax and enjoy life, while air can learn discipline in spending habits. However, this takes effort on the part of both spouses.

Sexually, the couple has to learn to listen to the other's particular needs. Earth tends to be a predictable lover, rarely full of surprises, while air, more imaginative and adventurous, loves unique and novel experiences. Therefore, earth can find air unsettling and erratic, while air may see earth as a stick-in-the-mud. However, earth is committed to pleasing his or her partner and will make great efforts to do so. A meeting in the middle is certainly possible, with earth playing air's erotic games on occasion, and air acquiescing to earth's need for stability.

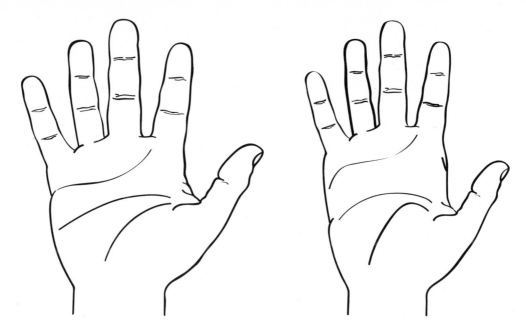

Figure 6-3: Earth hand/fire hand

Earth/Fire

Earth and fire (figure 6-3) are adversarial elements. Fire types and earth types work well together in the office place; the fire initiates the project and then turns it over to the earth, who finishes it diligently. Greco-romantically, however, this is an uncomfortable mix. Earth tends to be a bit too stable and predictable to hold a fire's attention for long, and to earth, fire is downright reckless!

Fire tends to be intense, driven, strong-willed, and passionate. Earth is calmer than fire, more relaxed and willing to work toward deferred rewards. Fire wants it now; earth has learned that anything worthwhile takes time. Serious conflicts can arise from this disparate way of achieving goals, especially in terms of parenting. Fire types can be strict disciplinarians, while earth types have a more easygoing, playful parenting style. If you know children who were pushed by their parents into becoming stressed overachievers, then you get the idea of fire-style parenting taken to the extreme.

Earth can exert a tempering influence on fire. Think of the difference between an out-of-control wildfire and a campfire contained by a ring of earth. Similarly, earth can provide fire with a degree of moderation and a sense of boundaries—just as long as earth doesn't make the mistake of trying to control fire. Fire hates overt attempts at control, but will recognize that some authoritative influence, as long as it isn't too heavy-handed, is probably a good thing.

The good news is that both earth and fire enjoy planning for success, and when the two put their minds together, truly awesome developments can result. Earth, seeing the big picture, can help fire with new and practical avenues to explore. Fire can inspire the earth to take more risks. Both partners will enjoy playing together, solving logic puzzles and word games, and an argument between them is like watching two chess masters at work as they try various strategies to gain the upper hand.

In terms of finance, both earth and fire see money as an important commodity, but for different reasons. Fire often measures his or her success by income, while earth sees money as a means of security. For an earth, success is measured in terms of peace of mind and satisfaction, while fire couldn't care less about a stress-free existence. Fire enjoys stress, as long as the payoff is worth the effort.

One of the important secrets in this match is the willingness to give each other plenty of room. Each partner will need occasional breaks from the other. Separate home offices, nights out with friends, or even the occasional separate vacation will help relieve some of the tension in this match.

The main sexual issue with earth and fire is timing. Fire arouses quickly, makes love in a frenzied whirlwind of passion, and afterward is likely to get up to work on a project. Earth, on the other hand, arouses gradually, makes love in a businesslike manner, and likes to talk and cuddle afterward. Both partners, if not careful, can experience constant frustration due to this out-of-sync manner of sexual expression.

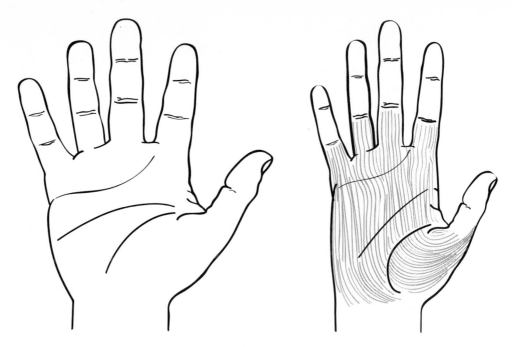

Figure 6-4: Earth hand/water hand

Earth/Water

Here is another complementary pairing (figure 6-4). Earth, the source from which all living things arise, and water, the natural nurturer, were made to be together. Both earth and water place the welfare of the family above all things, with earth providing the solid bedrock of the family and water seeing to the emotional well-being of family members.

Water types are somewhat passive, holding their secrets deeply and needing time to be alone and plumb the depths of their soul. Earth types are more involved in the world and like to stay in touch with what's going on, gathering information from news programs, informed experts, and personal experience.

Water is earth's personal cheerleader, helping build earth's self-esteem and encouraging him or her to go for the brass ring. Earth appreciates water's constant support and sees water as a safe haven for his or her emotional vulnerabilities. Both partners tend to open their hearts to each other, and the relationship has a tender sentimentality that's often remarked upon by others. This can be a "clingy" couple.

This relationship usually has strong mutual sexual attraction, but more than that, the couple builds a strong friendship that increases over the years, helping them weather the most tumultuous trials. Earth and water can tell each other anything and can count upon each other for tolerance, forgiveness, and understanding.

One potential area of friction arises when both partners are passionate about completely opposite subjects. Let's say, for example, that water wants to spend a sudden windfall on a European vacation while earth wants to add it to the retirement fund. When strong emotions arise between these two, there is a real danger of the discussion deteriorating into almost complete mutual misunderstanding. The more each partner tries to clarify his or her point of view, the more confused the communication becomes. In this case, earth and water combine to make mud, and as the old saying goes, "No amount of stirring can clear up a mud puddle." The frustration is not with the other party's lack of understanding, but rather, oddly enough, that each partner becomes frustrated because he or she wants to understand what the other is saying, but cannot. They both see this lack of comprehension as a personal failure, not the other person's fault. It's important in these conflicts for both parties to carefully choose words and express clearly his or her point of view.

I recall one earth/water couple who told me that the best way for them to communicate ideas to each other was through e-mail! Not a bad plan; the emotional detachment of written communication can help each partner carefully analyze what the other is thinking.

Sexually, this is a good match. Earth's gentle and affectionate lovemaking is balanced by water's emotionally responsive and empathetic surrender to the ebb and flow of erotic interplay. Sexual expression should be quite satisfying for both partners.

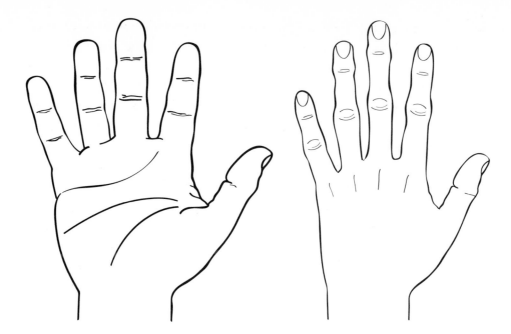

Figure 6-5: Earth hand/wood hand

Earth/Wood

These are two complementary elements (figure 6-5). Discussions between earth and wood are fascinating. Earth has a practical philosophy, while wood has a speculative philosophy. This leads to a discussion in which wood generates all kinds of solutions to the problem at hand while earth sifts through wood's ideas, distilling practical applications from the implausible. Earth often likes to stay within the box; wood sometimes doesn't even know that the box exists.

A strong mutual attraction between these elements leads over time to a deep understanding of each other's needs, moods, and preferences. Mutual acceptance and support are strong in this relationship. Earth, as noted, is practical, well-grounded and stable, qualities that wood holds in high regard. Earth admires wood's fluidity of thought and eloquent self-expression. One of the major differences between the two is wood's love of mental stimulation, new concepts, and intellectual speculation as opposed to earth's love of traditional, tried-and-true methods and strategies. The good news is that earth and wood are very tolerant of each other and seldom are threatened by the other's differences. Indeed, they cherish the divergences of opinion as a major contributing factor toward their success as a couple.

Romantically, the styles complement each other, because earth tends to get stuck in a rut of predictable behavior, while wood, ever curious, likes to explore new boundaries of experience. Mutual sensual massage is a terrific way for the two partners to ease into a lovemaking session, as they become attuned to each other's rhythms. Both earth and wood have an inner childlike quality that allows them to enjoy playing games and doing fun activities together, although earth has to feel secure in the relationship before this quality manifests in sexual play. In the bedroom, wood often says to earth, "Let's try this," suggesting some erotic variation he or she may have read about or thought up, and earth, with a smile both shy and at the same time mischievous, responds, "Okay."

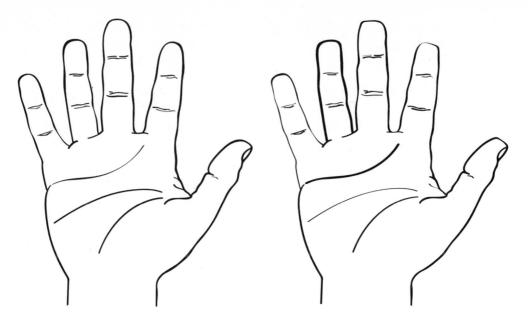

Figure 6-6: Earth hand/metal hand

Earth/Metal

Complementary elements, earth and metal (figure 6-6) both bring a businesslike drive to the relationship, taking care of the minutiae of daily life like two executives running a company. Both partners are strong, stubborn, and determined to succeed. Both earth and metal are doers, not talkers, so communication between them can be curt, brief, and to the point. What the relationship may lack in verbal communication it more than makes up for in the two partners' ability to work together toward a common goal. These two elements work well together on mundane, practical matters and make successful business partners as well as lovers.

Metal types aren't known for their sense of humor, while earth types have a teasing, mischievous quality. Sometimes metal types may think earth is making fun of him or her, while earth's only intention was to bring a little levity to the proceedings.

Metal often has a strong desire to plow through obstacles on his or her way to the finish line. Earth tends to be a bit more methodical, testing the water first before proceeding. These different approaches to time may be a potential source of friction, but since both partners usually are working in the same direction, conflict rarely escalates. It's more the case of earth urging metal to slow down, or metal trying to get past earth's natural caution and accelerate the proceedings.

Both earth and metal share a seemingly endless wellspring of energy and vitality, hating to sit around all day waiting for a lucky break. Both prefer to make things happen, rather than waiting on luck or fate. Neither likes to feel that success or happiness lies in anyone else's hands, and each partner encourages this independence in the other.

Metal types have an interesting anomaly in their personality. In public, they can be calm, almost aloof, and easily can be mistaken as frigid or unemotional. However, they are very good at concealing their intensity underneath a cool exterior. We get a clue of this in the outbursts of temper that occur occasionally with metal.

Sexually, metal tends to be aggressive, which earth can find pushy or, in some cases, breathtakingly exciting. Earth tends to finish sooner than metal, who at times can be well-nigh insatiable. Metal uses sexual activity to blow off the tension contained in that tightly controlled exterior. In the bedroom, metal can be uninhibited and over the top, incorporating all manner of props, costumes, or visual aids to enhance the sexual experience. Earth, swept away by this sexual intensity, goes along with whatever metal suggests due to an innate desire to please his or her lover. There's an almost addictive sexual magnetism between the two. Earth has to learn to keep up with metal, not only in daily affairs but in the bedroom as well.

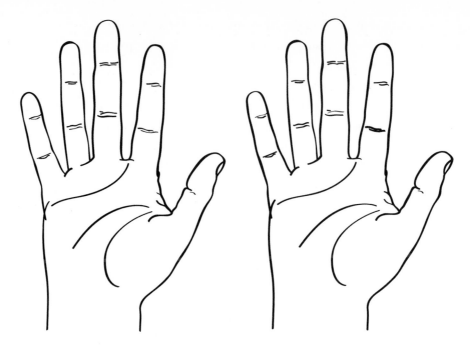

Figure 6-7: Air hand/air hand

Air/Air

As we've seen, two hands of the same element are always complementary. The air/air match (figure 6-7) is no exception, although there are a few areas of potential conflict that have to be addressed.

One of the true advantages of a same-element couple is that each person fully understands the other. Also, what one partner doesn't like about the other is a reflection of traits that he or she finds unattractive in him- or herself. Therefore, there is a constant feedback system that, over time, teaches each partner how to be the perfect companion for the other. Self-improvement is beneficial not only for each partner but for the overall relationship as well.

Air is an element that relishes intellectual and physical freedom, not doing well in tightly controlled conditions. Therefore, the air/air couple will be unusually free-spirited and open to new experiences. Air loves beauty, art, culture—any expression of the human spirit. Air can be childlike and unfettered, so each partner encourages the other to play games and have fun. Both partners are receptive, flexible, and creative, but also are inconsistent and at times moody, so the emotional flow of this couple can be erratic. However, once air commits to a relationship, he or she is extremely loyal and able to weather any storm.

Air is not always the most practical element, so the couple's lifestyle might seem chaotic and disorganized to some (earth and metal, for example). However, air can look at what appears to be random disorder and see a system that he or she perfectly understands. In that clutter, air always knows where everything is.

Air is not intrinsically good with finances, but can learn discipline in this area when required. Most air types will spend money freely, unless it's pointed out to them that there are such things in the world as rent, clothes, bills, etc.

Although on the surface air can appear flighty, it's dangerous to underestimate the intellectual power at the heart of the air element. There is a tremendous intelligence at the core, an insatiable curiosity that sometimes leads these people into unproductive tangents, but frequently allows them to see so far outside the box that they are true innovators. Therefore, their relationships often will be nontraditional and on the edge of the accepted norm. Sometimes it's difficult for air, a passive element, to take charge, so for an air/air couple, decision-making can become problematic. Each partner asks the other, "What do you want to do?" so many times that it can drive them to distraction.

Since air's idealism creates a tendency to see people and events as the air type wants them to be (as opposed to the way they really are), there is a danger that each partner will project a Greco-romanticized "image" of who they want their partner to be rather than who they really are. Two air types together can be, paradoxically, both naïve and insightful. Air types must learn to love the partner they have, complete with flaws and defects, rather than the partner they imagine in their head. They must avoid the temptation to escape into fantasy and constant introversion. When both air people learn to project their innate romantic nature onto the reality of the relationship, this can become one of the all-time legendary love affairs, the type that can inspire poets to compose sonnets.

Idealistic and romantic, each partner loves to delight the other with grand romantic gestures, like secluded getaways for anniversaries or an expensive gift that in reality neither one can afford. Conversely, air types can be equally moved by small gestures, such as an apple with a smiley face drawn on it or a scrap of poetry. For the air, it's definitely the thought that counts. If this seems contradictory, well—that's air.

The sexual expression of air embraces an incredible range, moving from gentle, breezy, and languorous lovemaking to frenzied hurricanes of passion, quickly aroused and just as quickly spent. Many air couples, with their mutual desire for change and variety, prefer an "open" relationship to the closed custom of monogamy. Air types are dramatic, sometimes frustrating, and intuitively creative, but never, ever boring.

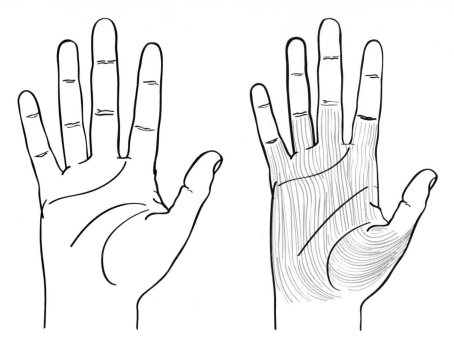

Figure 6-8: Air hand/water hand

Air/Water

Oddly enough, I've found that the strongest initial sexual attraction occurs between antagonistic elements. Complementary elements usually are mildly attracted to each other at first, like a friendship, and the attraction grows over time. It sneaks up on them, and one day they become aware, somewhat to their surprise, that they're in love!

Air and water (figure 6-8) are antagonistic elements, so at first they will be strongly attracted to each other. Each will yearn to possess the other. However, after the initial heat wears off, they will have to take an objective look at the relationship to see if there is a solid foundation upon which to build. Often there is, but sometimes there's not, and the two then will have to face a hard fact: the ride was great fun while it lasted, but now it's time to part.

However, if the two can find solid ground upon which to build a relationship, then even antagonistic elements can flourish together. Humans are, if nothing else, extremely resilient, and a relationship can be founded upon a small kernel of shared goals, interests, or even a similar taste in movies. Building on shared similarities, the couple uses the points of divergence as a source of dynamic energy. What could be a repelling force instead becomes strongly attractive.

Air and water are the fundamental elements of a storm, so the relationship will be tempestuous and passionate and will move very quickly. Think of a "whirlwind relationship" and you get the idea. Consequently, when tempers flare, the storm blows over quickly—but some dishes might have to be replaced.

It says in the Tao Te Ching that strong winds do not blow all morning, nor do strong rains fall all day. In order for this coupling to succeed, the gale-force energies have to be tamed to a steady breeze. This tends to happen over time; the older we get, the less interested we are in precipitating stressful situations. We learn to let go of issues that really aren't worth the emotional investment and to save our energies for more productive ventures.

Sexually, this is a volatile couple. Sometimes hot, sometimes cold, this couple may experience long periods of sexual abstinence followed by days of frantic lovemaking. The relationship is cyclic, like the seasons, and many air/water couples break up early in the relationship. If they hang on, however, they begin to understand the cyclic nature of their relationship and learn to weather the periodic storms.

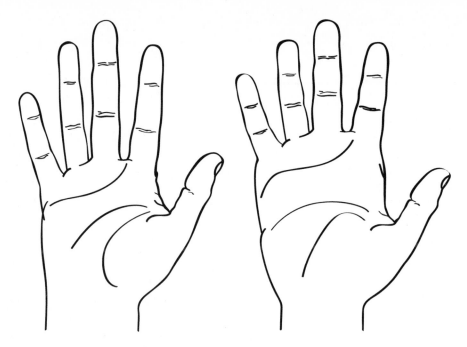

Figure 6-9: Air hand/fire hand

Air/Fire

These are complementary elements (figure 6-9). Air responds enthusiastically to fire's impulsive nature and intense emotional expression, often saying outrageous things just to see how fire will react. Fire is receptive to air's quick, agile mind and enjoys acting as a sounding board for air's mental excursions.

Both air and fire are free spirits who chafe under too many restrictions—they both need room to spread their wings. Consequently, both can have trouble with authority, fire being openly rebellious and air being more passive-aggressive. Both air and fire love travel, meeting people, and staying abreast of current world affairs. Neither cares very much about what's popular, conventional, or in style, preferring to do their own thing in their own way. Neither needs the approval of everyone else to feel secure about themselves.

Air explores possibilities, looking at an issue from every available angle. Fire, on the other hand, is quick, opinionated, decisive, and prone to snap decisions. Although air and fire have some opposing traits in their respective personalities, they both are attracted to the things in their partner that they lack. Air admires fire's to-the-point approach, and fire enjoys air's unique perspective on things.

Because of their mutual intellectual attraction, air and fire engage in in-depth dialogue during which they unlock their innermost secret feelings, goals, and insecurities. This leads to a deep, trusting relationship with mutual support. After all, fire needs air in order to burn, and air is most comfortable when it's warm.

Fire's strong sexual needs are easily matched by air; no matter how long the fire burns, there's always plenty of air to keep it stoked. Fire is usually the instigator of lovemaking, though air has sneaky ways to plant the idea in fire's head. With fire's passion and air's imagination, there are no boundaries in the bedroom. Sexual exploration is carried to new levels by a fire/air couple. They have to remind themselves sometimes to take it easy, or they'll overdo it to the point of exhaustion. Due to the danger of fire and air becoming obsessed with each other, it's a good idea for them to take an occasional break from their relationship.

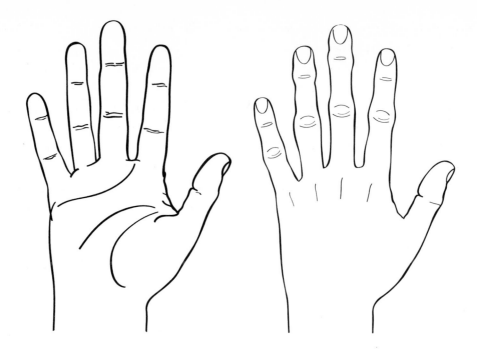

Figure 6-10: Air hand/wood hand

Air/Wood

Wood and air (figure 6-10) are complementary elements. Both are cerebral elements that share many similarities in their approach to life. Both are dreamers, though wood tends to be a more disciplined dreamer than air, if that makes sense. Wood dreams about goals that can be attained logically, while air has no problem with the idea that magic can happen if you let it. Both air and wood are sensitive to possibilities, growth potentials, and new avenues of relationship dynamics to explore. Both are eager to learn from the other.

Air and wood will enjoy experiencing music, art, literature, and other cultural activities together, each bringing their own unique perspective into the experience. Air and wood types usually have creative self-expression of their own, which they share with the other partner for feedback. Wood has to be careful not to be too critical of air, who can be terribly sensitive about the fruits of his or her creativity.

You can see the differences in the two intellectual styles while observing the wood/air interaction with other people. Wood enjoys the company of others, especially intellectually interesting people with diverse collections of ideas and opinions. Wood enjoys lively conversation and debate with these groups. Air, on the other hand, likes to sit and observe the activities and conversations of others, often maintaining an internal running commentary. In other words, while wood likes to be part of the picture, air sometimes prefers being the frame. Air is accepting of most people's points of view, but wood, which is extremely analytical and critical, can be intolerant of views that are illogical or irrational. To an air type, just because something is illogical doesn't mean it's not useful. This can be a potential source of conflict for the couple when they're discussing plans involving their future security.

Both wood and air are terrific psychologists, finding endless enjoyment in analyzing a person's inner motivations and psychological underpinnings. Air does this more intuitively and quickly than wood, who prefers a logical, step-by-step approach. The couple usually forms a deep understanding of each other in a very short span of time. The wood/air relationship has elements of deep trust and friendship; even when they break up, they often remain best friends.

There is an amusing fact about most wood/air couples: wood usually thinks that he or she is the intellectual light of the family, when in reality the air partner is almost always smarter. Air types just don't broadcast their true potential, preferring to hide their keen intellect under a slightly flighty exterior. These people will allow others to underestimate them to their advantage. Air types are also a bit manipulative, so if it suits their purpose to allow wood to think he or she is smarter, they encourage that belief.

Sexually, wood and air go through phases, sometimes making love urgently and frequently and sometimes simply enjoying each other's company with very little sexual activity. Both are stimulated by the outdoors, so a cabin getaway is a good way to fan dormant flames. Air and wood, unfortunately, have bad timing together in the bedroom, as well as out-of-sync moods and goals. Wood is almost obsessively punctual, while the dreamy air is seldom on time for anything. This isn't too serious but can be irritating.

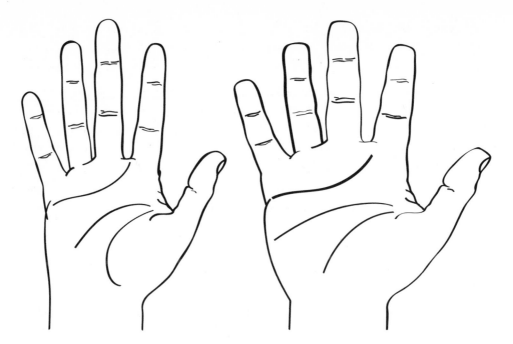

Figure 6-11: Air hand/metal hand

Air/Metal

With their antagonistic elements, the air/metal couple (figure 6-11) have their work cut out for them. Metal is controlling, finicky, and perfectionistic, while air prefers a more freewheeling and casual lifestyle. Obviously, these are fertile grounds for dissatisfaction, as metal becomes frustrated with air's relaxed way of doing things, and air chafes under metal's constant insistence on controlled perfection. Metal lacks air's ability to analyze his or her partner's needs, so if the air wants something from metal, it does no good to hint: air has to come out and ask for it.

To ease the tension with metal, air has to learn routines for daily tasks, such as picking up around the house and putting everything where it belongs. The problem is that air is not a creature of habit. Routines and repetitive patterns tend to bore air, who likes to perform the same task in as many different ways as possible. Metal plows through obstacles, goals, and relationship issues, while air likes to digress and explore all the possibilities his or her agile mind detects. Metal simply does not understand this; to a metal, if something works, don't mess with it, and for goodness' sake stick to the point! Metal's lesson is to understand air's peculiar ways and learn to let go of piddling issues that really don't matter in the long run.

There is a strong tendency in this relationship toward anger, argumentativeness, and abusive words and actions. The couple's communication styles are completely different, so each partner has to learn to speak the language of the other. Metal is logical and to the point, while air speaks in metaphors, with strong emotional content. Air and metal will enjoy challenging each other's viewpoints and ideas, and it's important to conduct these exchanges mindfully lest they escalate into angry confrontation. Equally important is for each partner to avoid coercion through forcing his or her views on the other. Air and metal are independent thinkers, each in his or her own way, and will not tolerate attempts at intellectual control.

Sexually, there can be issues, because air and metal have different ways of expressing erotic behavior. Air types tend to be free and uninhibited, surrendering themselves to the sensual flow, while metal types need to be coaxed out of their inner cave.

Like the Tin Man, you wonder if metal lacks a heart. Metal seems aloof and unexpressive on the surface, but usually has deep and intense feelings that rarely show through. It's not that the tender feelings are nonexistent; it's just that metal distrusts feelings and wants to subject them to a thorough analysis before allowing them to fly from the coop. So in the bedroom, metal needs time to relax and let go of his or her inhibitions. Usually, the first sexual episode is a little awkward, the second better, and the third one quite satisfactory. Some preliminary relaxation activities, such as nonsexual massage, can lead to something a little hotter.

The advantage in this relationship goes to air, the master psychologist, who learns devious ways to push metal's emotional buttons and allow the trapped emotions to push free. Sometimes this is a relief for metal, but sometimes he or she resents it. It takes time to know when to poke metal and when to leave well enough alone.

A friend of mine who is a metal came to visit me for a few days a week after his mother's death. For the first couple of days he spoke of the funeral as though it had happened to someone else or was something he saw on television; he was detached, factual, noncommittal. Having known this fellow since childhood, I waited, asking questions to keep him talking. I knew it was only a matter of time until he would feel comfortable enough with me to say what was really on his mind. One evening while he was talking of something else—hockey, of all things—his face twitched. I knew what was happening, so I moved a little closer to him. It took three days, but the deeply repressed grief eventually poured out.

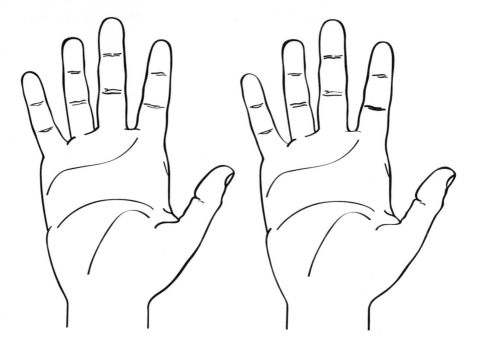

Figure 6-12: Fire hand/fire hand

Fire/Fire

This is a compatible mating (figure 6-12), but may not seem so to outside observers due to the explosive nature of the relationship, resulting in flare-ups and passionate disagreements. There are many literary works devoted to married couples who have taken domestic discord to the level of a martial art; *The Lion in Winter* and *Who's Afraid of Virginia Woolf?* come to mind. I've always felt that these were textbook examples of a fire/fire relationship left unattended, blazing out of control. However, there is hope for this couple. A cooperative fire coupling can be a beautiful thing to behold, like fireworks in a clear sky.

Fire types evoke extremely intense emotional reactions from each other and have strong and sometimes opposing opinions, which can lead to simultaneous attraction and repulsion toward each other. Blowups can occur not only over big issues like trust, jealousy, and lack of consideration for each other's feelings, but also over seemingly trivial events such as forgetting to take out the trash or leaving the cap off the toothpaste. The couple is capable of quite dramatic emotional extremes, going from powerful passion for one another to boiling anger. However, they stick together due to the fierce love and attraction they feel for each other. There is an obsessive quality to this relationship, and it's not uncommon for fire types to stay together until death separates them.

The double fire couple, more than any other same-element pairing, have to learn to cool down and be more objective about things. A long relationship is probable, just as it always is with identical elements, but the degree of stress and tension can be minimized with a little understanding and insight into one another's expectations. Otherwise, the relationship will dissolve into an endless series of power struggles.

Fire types enjoy physical and athletic activities together, but can become competitive with each other. When on the same page concerning finance, parenting, and marital goals, the couple can be energetic and untiring, spurring each other to express his or her strongest qualities. Fire types challenge each other to deeply examine internal beliefs, boundaries, and habits, so the couple's joint performance is marked by excellence.

Sexually, this couple is, as you might expect, hot. Arousing quickly to the boiling point, their lovemaking is frenzied, loud, and sometimes violent, leading to scratches and even bruises. Arguments, oddly enough, can be delicious foreplay for the fire/fire couple. They enjoy playful S & M and often are delighted by romantic encounters in public places. Fire's motto: the more danger, the more excitement. I usually caution this couple to be careful so they won't be arrested.

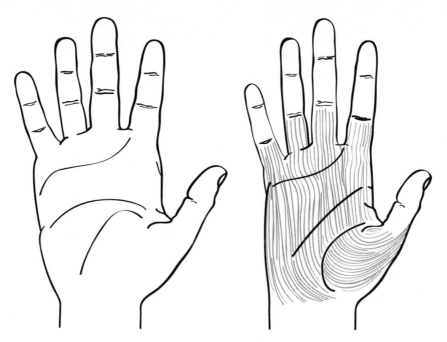

Figure 6-13: Fire hand/water hand

Fire/Water

Fire and water (figure 6-13) are antagonistic elements, so conflict can be expected. However, the arguments rage intently for a short while and then evaporate completely, leaving the air clear. Think of throwing a cupful of water onto a hot fire: a burst of steam, then calm.

Both fire and water have an instinctive drive to stay busy and on the go. Consequently, this couple will have a low tolerance for tedium and boredom. The relationship has to have variety and momentum and be filled with interesting activities. Frequent vacations usually are helpful.

Water is focused on the present and can let the past go as long as the present moment is enjoyable and secure. Fire, however, can carry a grudge forever. Letting go of emotional issues is not fire's strongest suit. In this couple, water has to learn to let things go, as fire has difficulty letting go of a grudge. As the saying goes, holding a grudge is like taking poison hoping someone else will die. Anger never hurts the other person but undermines our own peace of mind. Fire has to learn this lesson or be doomed to carry a lifelong burden of resentment. It can be done; it's just particularly difficult for fire.

Both fire and water love new experiences, so the couple will pick up interests together, enjoy them intensely for a while and then letting them go when they both decide the activity has outlived its usefulness. The problem is in timing: fire tends to set activities aside as soon as boredom sets in, while water prefers to explore a subject in depth and experience as much of its potential as possible. This can cause the couple to move apart in two totally opposite directions.

Fire likes to start projects but sometimes is weak on the follow-up. Fire likes immediate gratification, while water can wait for a result, as long as the payoff is sufficient to justify the wait. Water, being nurturing, likes to cultivate even the most tenuous project through to completion. This can be a possible source of conflict but with attention can become a terrific cooperative asset for the long-term relationship. Some issues require decisive action (fire) while some require contemplation (water). Together, the fire/water couple covers all the bases.

As is true of all pairings involving antagonistic elements, this relationship is complex and often contradictory. Fire and water find each other fascinating and extremely attractive, especially in the sexual sense. Over time, however, fire and water can become uncomfortable with each other's personality differences, deeply ingrained ways of doing things, and political and spiritual attitudes. During conversation, fire can be abrupt, terse, and to the point, while water sometimes takes a circuitous route to get to the point. During such conversations, fire becomes frustrated with water's seemingly endless circumlocutions. Meanwhile, water sees fire as abrupt, impatient, and insensitive.

Like all relationships between antagonistic elements, tolerance and patience are the most important skills to bring to the table. Water must learn that fire sometimes has little interest in rambling conversation, while fire has to recognize water's tendency to want to go very deeply into a subject. If this conflict can be balanced, fire finds water to be a terrific source of unconventional approaches, and fire's natural impulsiveness can become, over time, more considered and controlled.

Sexually speaking, this is a hot combination. Fire can scorch through the layers of water and bring out the most intense passion. Water's empathetic response excites fire and, just as when an amount of water meets an equal amount of fire, steam erupts. There are some potential sexual conflicts to pay attention to: Fire enjoys quick arousal and strong stimulation (like biting and scratching) and usually climaxes quickly and explosively. Water, on the other hand, likes to linger over lovemaking and enjoys languorous foreplay, affectionate touching, cuddling, and pillow talk. The two styles could not be more different, and this requires attention if the couple wants to have a mutually satisfying love life.

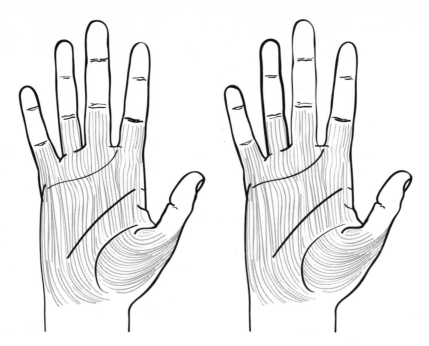

Figure 6-14: Water hand/water hand

Water/Water

There is an almost painfully tender aspect to the water/water relationship (figure 6-14). Water is the empathetic element, and when two water types get together, the mutual sympathy and compassion forge a bond that is close, mystical, and a true merging of souls. When you combine two drops of water, you don't get two separate drops—you produce one bigger drop. It's impossible to delineate where one drop ends and the other begins. Each partner merges emotionally with the other and actually feels whatever the other experiences. This merging leads to a deep, intuitive, and magical understanding of each other.

Water, being nurturing, ensures that the couple will focus on each other's well-being. Often, the couple becomes so intent on focusing on each other's needs that everyone else is excluded from the relationship. This can increase the feelings of security and belonging, but over time may begin to feel too restricting. Water types have to be careful not to isolate themselves from other family members and friends.

Water is a restless element and has to flow freely or it will stagnate. If not allowed some freedom of movement, the two water types eventually will begin to get on each other's nerves. But is it not as simple as that: the two may find, paradoxically, that the more they irritate each other, the more the attraction between them increases. If you stir water into water, you get more water.

Remember that water is the most changeable of elements, so it can manifest as gas, liquid, or solid. Due to this shapeshifting quality, a water/water relationship is never simple, never black and white, but is always multisided and complex. It's one of the more nuanced couplings; to an outsider it may appear complex, paradoxical, and chaotic. Outsiders may even see a water/water coupling as a meeting of opposites, but this is an illusion due to water's shapeshifting abilities. Water types react to each other on an intuitive level, often experiencing inspiration, bursts of insight, and passionate zeal. The intensity of emotion can lead to withdrawal and sullenness, but water understands that this is only surface tension, not deep resentment.

Water is an intuitive, psychic element, so each partner can virtually read the other's mind, which makes deception impossible. Even when separated from their partner, water types can sense when their beloved is hurt, angry, or in danger. There are too many stories to recount about water types knowing their partner had been in an accident, though separated by hundreds of miles. This happens far too often to be chalked up to coincidence.

If water isn't careful, he or she can become too serious about life, and a water/water couple can become too serious about each other. Two water types together can produce an introverted, serious relationship that excludes spontaneity and playfulness. This should be watched for and corrected. Fun holidays together are a necessity, in my opinion, to let the waters explore each other's mutual playfulness.

Sexually, two waters understand each other so well, on all levels, that they surrender to the waves and eddies of sensuality, merging to form one undulating and totally united being. For water, lovemaking is a spiritual act, a coming together of two souls, a communion. Sometimes the lovemaking seems to lack overt passion, but the spiritual connection makes the joining of two water types very, very deep.

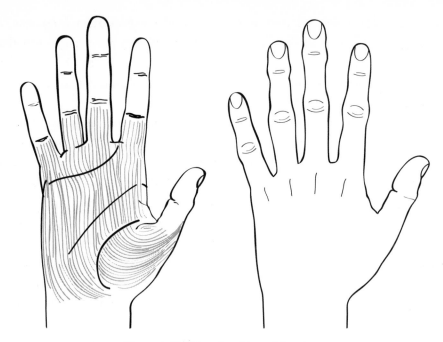

Figure 6-15: Water hand/wood hand

Water/Wood

Complementary elements, both wood and water (figure 6-15) are intellectually deep and have complex, multilevel minds and a seemingly endless capacity for adapting to new situations. Therefore, this couple rides well together through periods of stress. There commonly is an age difference in this couple, the wood partner being several years older than the water partner.

This is one of the more romantic couplings. Both partners have an idealistic personality, which they bring to every aspect of the relationship, from romance and sexuality to day-to-day existence. Both are good at adjusting to the other's quirks. They see each other as a mystery to be solved and love to spend time together experimenting and exploring each other's interests and boundaries. Wood's practical intellect appeals to water's need for a secure vessel, and water's wonderful empathy makes water a safe haven for wood's well-concealed emotional insecurities. The relationship probably sprang into being spontaneously and impulsively, almost by magic, and this element of spontaneity will flourish throughout the duration of the relationship.

However, this mutual romanticism is not always ideal. Too much romanticizing can lead to a fantasy-based relationship, with a mutual denial of the challenging issues that spring up within even the most compatible mating. Belief in a fairy tale relationship can cause the couple to sweep potential problems under the carpet and refuse to admit that life with another, even a beloved other, is sometimes hard.

Wood, in its desire to study water, will push water's buttons to see what happens. Water can find this irritating, assuming that wood is deliberately teasing and prodding. Water is prone to passive resistance in this relationship and can respond to wood's teasing with sullen withdrawal. Wood usually doesn't have a clue what he or she did to spark this resentment. Wood can be objective, almost clinical at times, when dealing with relationship issues, sometimes lacking empathy. The more empathetic and emotional water finds wood's intellectual objectivity hard to understand.

Wood is good at deducing another person's feelings but sometimes is remarkably out of touch with his or her own. Water's intuitive probing can ferret out emotional issues of which wood was unaware. Therefore, this can be a healing relationship for both partners, an adventure in self-discovery.

Sex between water and wood is deep, mystical, and emotionally enveloping. Water surrounds wood with sensuality and sweeps the breathless wood away to drown in water's emotional energy. The couple will enjoy role-playing and incorporating props and accessories into their bed play. Wood loves to teach his or her partner the more exotic and refined techniques of lovemaking, and water is an apt and attentive pupil who absorbs the new information eagerly. In between voyages of sexual exploration, both will enjoy lingering over foreplay, touching and caressing each other to prolong the pleasure as long as they can stand it.

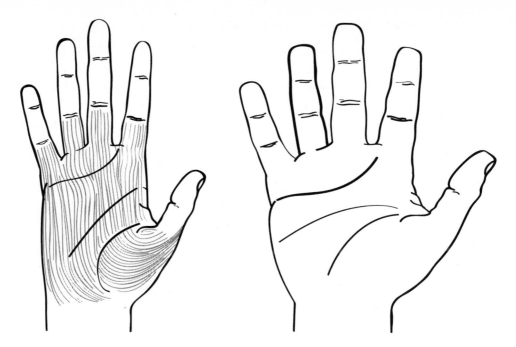

Figure 6-16: Water hand/metal hand

Water/Metal

Water and metal (figure 6-16) are complementary elements, which surprises a lot of people. We usually think of water causing metal to disintegrate into rust, but it's actually air that corrodes metal through oxidation. Water can precipitate this reaction, but it's air that finishes the job.

How can empathetic, nurturing water be compatible with rigid, stolid metal? Well, at the inner core of metal is an insecure, childlike quality to which water feels drawn. Water, the deep element, can sense the hidden depths of others and is not fooled by metal's protective emotional exoskeleton. Water yearns to cradle and protect that insecure being, and metal, gently coaxed out of his or her shell, welcomes the protective and nurturing love that water so generously provides.

This is a good match. Metal's businesslike approach and water's emotional nurturing ensure that their children are well cared for both materially and emotionally. Metal provides a secure chalice in which water happily resides, and from this secure base water has a safe haven to which he or she can return after the demands of the day have been met.

I've said that the parenting styles of water and earth differ. Let me go into more detail. If a child goes to a parent who's a water with a problem, he or she can expect sympathy, compassion, and emotional support. If the child takes the same problem to a parent who's a metal, he or she will receive a tactical, systematic analysis of the situation and focused strategies on how to resolve it. Family meetings chaired by water are like psychological counseling sessions; when they're led by metal, it's more like a tactical military conference or the point-by-point agenda of a business seminar. This is why water and metal make such a strong parenting team: by the time their children reach adulthood, they have received emotional nurturing as well as a full toolkit of how to deal with life's most demanding tasks.

Metal types, oddly enough, are deeply insecure about relationships. They won't say anything about this, but will sometimes test their partner to see if he or she still loves them. Water's intuition senses that metal occasionally needs reassurance and will rise to the occasion, performing loving gestures or otherwise showing his or her devotion. Metal types tend to value actions over words, so telling them that you love them isn't always enough; you have to show them. Water, however, can spot insincerity in a heartbeat, so if you tell a water that you love him or her, you'd better mean it.

In the bedroom, metal is aggressive and likes to takes charge of the situation. Water—supple, flexible, yielding, but never passive—allows metal to think he or she is in control. Sex between these two is a game played on many levels, emotional, intellectual, and physical. Over time, metal begins to wonder if he or she really is the one in control, or if water is gradually shaping him or her over time. Remember, given enough time, water can erode mountains into valleys. Eventually, the successful water/metal couple reaches an elemental joining in which water flows into metal's interior, filling him or her up like you would an empty bottle. Water has found a way through metal's defenses, and metal welcomes the penetration into his or her well-protected inner sanctum. But it does take time and willingness for both parties to do the work. Water has an almost supernatural patience with metal, so as time passes, water finds the hidden crevasses and passages that run deep into the metal's heart. Since these are compatible elements, this is easily accomplished. Despite their apparent differences, water and metal instinctively like each other.

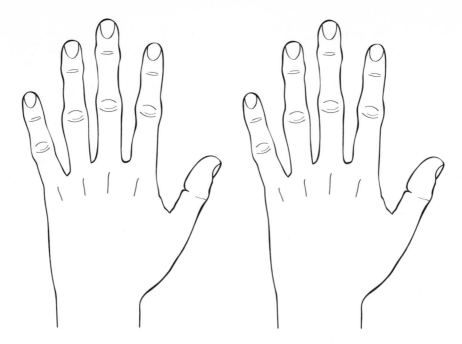

Figure 6-17: Wood hand/wood hand

Wood/Wood

Wood and wood (figure 6-17) have an intellectually deep understanding of what it takes to forge a solid commitment. When two philosophers get together, a free and unlimited exchange of ideas can be expected. This couple sees a relationship as a foundation upon which to build something bigger than the two of them: a spiritual commitment to a higher ideal. Each partner will be capable of sacrifice, patience, and determination to reach this ideal that they both see within their grasp. Communication seldom is a problem; both are quite eloquent and in touch with their needs. Typically, wood is capable of giving more information than you really need, so don't ask unless you really want to know.

Because of this mutual spirituality, it's important for the wood/wood couple to share a similar spiritual view of the world. A mismatch in this area can be disastrous. Imagine an atheist living with a devout Christian, for example. Unless both partners are equally skilled in practicing denial, there's going to be trouble. This is twice as true with the wood/wood mating, because ideals and values are extremely important components of wood's sense of self, and wood can become quite defensive once arriving at an intellectual conclusion.

Wood types can be a bit moody, since their philosophical inquiries involve a lot of self-analysis. They ask the big questions: Who am I? Why am I here? What is the purpose of the universe? These questions prod awake the demons sleeping in wood's subconscious. Two wood types together tend to lock into each other's emotional cycles, so when one is emotionally down, the other will follow. Conversely, when one wood is experiencing an epiphany or joy, the other wood is right there with him or her.

This is an extremely compatible couple in the bedroom. Wood types like voyeuristic activities, so costuming and role-playing will be powerful turn-ons for this couple. Wood types also love to experiment in the bedroom, so a wood/wood couple is twice as likely as any other couple to push the boundaries of sexual expression. Some of these experiments lead to comical and sometimes disastrous results, while others yield surprisingly enjoyable outcomes. After lovemaking, wood types like to lie together and talk about various subjects, read, or watch interesting movies.

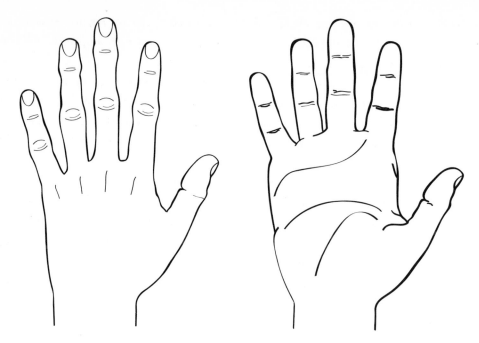

Figure 6-18: Wood hand/fire hand

Wood/Fire

Wood and fire (figure 6-18) are probably the most obvious antagonistic elements. After all, you just have to look at the news to see what devastation a wildfire can inflict on a forest. However, fire combined with wood also makes a campfire, something to keep away the wolves and the winter chill.

In nature, the relationship between fire and wood is symbiotic: Fire clings to wood and draws sustenance from it. Once the supply of wood is exhausted, fire ceases to exist. A steady supply of wood is necessary for fire's continued existence. Wood can exist without fire, but fire cannot exist without fuel. This is a good metaphor for the relationship between a wood/fire couple: fire tends to consume wood until wood is exhausted. Thus, the secret to making this pairing work is to know just how much of oneself to give at a time. Any time we go to extremes, we're acting unwisely, so moderation is a good watchword for us all; but it's an especially important practice for this couple. Too much fire and wood is consumed; too much wood and fire is smothered. Just the right amount of each and the home fires burn steadily.

In a heated discussion, fire tends to flare up and become passionate. Wood becomes uncomfortable with fire's heat and retreats behind a façade of didacticism and logic—which, of course, frustrates fire, and the heat escalates. Left to soar out of control, fire blazes. Wood then retreats, and the end result is a lot of anger. Communication skills are a must for this couple. As with all antagonistic elements, each must learn to speak the language of the other.

As it turns out, my parents were a wood/fire couple. They would argue passionately for hours and then disappear into the bedroom, where the passion turned from argumentiveness into something quite different. Their marriage lasted for twenty-five years, and this heat never abated. My dad's fire fed upon my mom's inexhaustible supply of wood, and we children were puzzled by how two people who fought so passionately could love each other so deeply. Life is certainly an adventure, and love one of its most enduring mysteries.

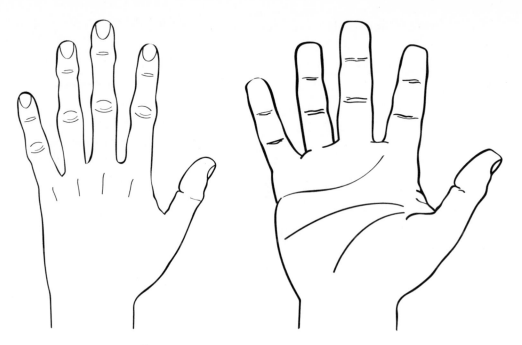

Figure 6-19: Wood hand/metal hand

Wood/Metal

These two are antagonistic elements (figure 6-19). Just as metal tools are used to chop down trees and whittle wood into different shapes, so does the metal partner attempt to strip down the wood partner and reshape him or her into a new form, one the metal approves of. Wood's independent spirit resists this, and the source of conflict is obvious. Metal tends to dominate this relationship, seeing wood's intellectual resistance as a sign of waning affection and a threat to the security of the relationship. Though tough on the outside, metal is an insecure element and sometimes blows perceived rejection out of proportion. There's a danger of metal becoming critical of wood's favorite activities, cultural tastes, and family and friends.

Metal and wood have different strategies in selecting and maintaining friendships. Metal usually practices the "winner" mentality, selecting his or her friends from those with similar competitive attitudes. Wood likes interesting people with exotic and radical lifestyles and doesn't really care how successful the person is in terms of money or power. Typically, wood's friends encompass a wide range of free-thinking characters, from comic-book aficionados, magicians, actors, and symphonic musicians to theoretical physicists and authors. Metal sees little use in impractical activities and can become critical of wood's friends.

So can this couple survive? Yes, for several reasons. An element rarely exists in pure form. A metal type with an infusion of earth or wood can call upon these additional traits to find common ground with wood. Hands actually change over time, although the shape of the hand is the part that changes the slowest. It takes a lot of work and willpower to change the basic pattern of our personality. However, if we diligently discourage unpleasant states as they arise in the mind and cultivate desirable traits, then over time we refine and purify our minds. Metal types have a keen and observant intellect, and when they see that certain behaviors are counterproductive, they'll usually abandon them. Metal is very motivated by the "payoff," both in business and personal life, and will do whatever is necessary to achieve the desired result.

Another factor in favor of this couple is that wood is an exceptionally tolerant and flexible element. It has to be, or it will break. Think of a tree swaying in high winds. If the tree didn't give with the wind, it would be uprooted and swept away. This is why wood types are usually Jacks-of-all-trades. They want to master every subject and are flexible enough to adapt to the circumstances of any situation in which they find themselves. This is also why wood types sometimes are seen by more "practical" people as unfocused and lacking discipline, which is a spectacular misjudgment.

Sometimes you have to wonder how certain couples got together in the first place, but it happens all the time. Since the metal/wood partners saw something in each other that was worth further involvement, there have to be mutual reasons to work on the relationship. They just have to find the seed of compatibility and nurture it into full flower.

The main sexual issue for this couple is that metal and wood have different expectations concerning the act of lovemaking. Metal sees sex as a necessary function, like eating or going to the bathroom, while wood considers sex a metaphor for the relationship itself. If the lovemaking is good and mutually satisfying, wood sees this as an indication that the relationship is on track. Rather than viewing sex as a barometer, metal focuses on whether the relationship meets certain practical guidelines: are we on the same page regarding finance, children, long-term plans? Wood sees sex as a medicine to heal stress between the couple. If metal feels insecure in his or her daily existence, then sex is the last thing on his or her mind.

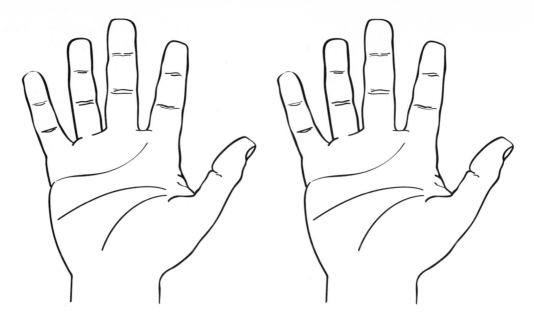

Figure 6-20: Metal hand/metal hand

Metal/Metal

Extremely complementary, two metals (figure 6-20) together can accomplish anything—just dare them to do it or say that it's impossible and then watch them go. Metal types tend to keep emotions private, so to outside observers the couple may seem to lack spontaneous affection. This can be an illusion. Within the protective security of a trusting relationship, the metal partners welcome each other into their inner emotional vaults where outsiders are never allowed.

The metal/metal partners will have similar tastes in friends, activities, and lifestyle goals, so friction between the two is minimal. They may become patrons of the arts or support local charitable agencies. They set mutual goals, plan their strategies on how to achieve these goals together, and work diligently to obtain the desired results.

Metal is a very private element, so the metal/metal partners give out precious few clues concerning their emotional and sexual life. To outsiders, this marriage is a closed vault. While the metal/metal partners enjoy group activities, they really let their hair down only when in the company of each other. Neither partner will be clingy, as each respects the autonomy and independence of the other. A relation based on constant to-getherness suits a water/water pair but not a metal/metal couple. Each partner has the freedom to make his or her own decisions, live his or her own life, and pursue his or her own goals. The relationship will be unusually open, free, and nonpossessive, with few strings attached. Each trusts the other's sense of responsibility to do whatever needs to be accomplished.

Metal is an independent element that dislikes being bossed around or controlled by anyone. Since metal likes to be in control, when a metal/metal couple have a difference in opinion, it can lead to an uncomfortable stalemate. Naturally competitive even with each other, neither partner will want to concede his or her position. Both partners are proud, have large egos, and dislike admitting weakness or error. Compromise will not come easily under these conditions. Having two bosses in the same relationship can be problematic on occasion. It's vital for the happiness of these partners that they place less emphasis on independence and work on the nurturing elements of their relationship. Otherwise, they will begin to see each other as competitive rivals, rather than two people who are on the same team.

In the bedroom, the metal/metal couple have a businesslike interest in pleasing each other. They believe that you get back what you put in, so they work toward understand-ing the other's needs and learning to satisfy them.

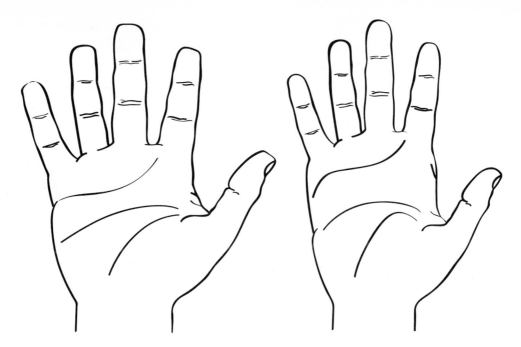

Figure 6-21: Metal hand/fire hand

Metal/Fire

Metal and fire (figure 6-21) are antagonistic. Of all the elements, fire has the best chance of conquering metal in a battle of wills. Fire accelerates the corrosive effect of air on metal, so these elements are volatile when brought together. Fire inflames metal, sometimes to the point of meltdown, and fire sees metal's aloofness as a challenge.

However, people have free will, something that raw elements in nature seem to lack. Therefore, metal can draw a great deal of inspiration from fire's passion. Likewise, fire can melt metal's steely exterior and unlock emotions, passions, and motivations that metal had no idea were there. It can be a somewhat violent process, but is ultimately productive.

As I've pointed out, sometimes the strongest initial attraction seems to be between antagonistic elements. When fire and metal come together, the heavens ring. It's like the two metal hemispheres of an atomic bomb slamming together and producing a plume of fiery energy. The fire/metal combination makes for hot affairs, but when striving for longevity, a couple needs more than the momentum of an initial mutual attraction to stay together. There have to be compromise, understanding, and patience, none of which come easily to either metal or fire. However, both are high-powered achievers when they want to be, so anything is possible. If the partners sense that something special exists between them, some underlying magic that can be kindled into full-blown love, then they will work strenuously to cultivate the relationship no matter how much friction is raised along the way.

The compatibility profiles discussed in this chapter can help us understand the essential styles and strategies of each couple. In the next chapter we'll combine all the techniques we've learned so far to draw a picture of our ideal lover.

chapter seven

Putting the Pieces Together: Tips on Spotting Your Ideal Lover

I've been informed by people skeptical of psychic matters that all psychics do is tell people what they want to hear. I wish this were true, but I often find myself in the position of having to tell people that the outcome of their specific situation is probably not going to be what they wish, or tell a couple that the differences between them are probably irresolvable. I truly dislike this unpleasant aspect of my work, but people come to me seeking my objective and professional opinion. It would be a disservice both to my craft and my clients to offer anything less than what I feel is the truth.

From the moment we're born and up to the moment we die, we have to contend with that great beast—*reality*—also known as *The Way Things Are*. During our lives, we're constantly constructing a set of expectations, hopes, and assumptions that we refine and add to for the rest of our lives. These assumptions and deductions include our experiences, opinions, observations, lessons learned from teachers and parents, and whatever religious and philosophical dogma we care to mix in for flavor. This process of creation results in a package of mental constructs that we'll call *The Way We Want Things to Be*. Here's the point: between the gap that exists between The Way Things Are and The Way We Want Things to Be is all the suffering in the world, and I mean that literally.

For the time being, we'll set aside physical suffering and concentrate on emotional suffering, mental states that we experience as stress. Stress is the tension between the way the world is and the way we want it to be. The bigger the gap between these two extremes, the more stress is experienced. For example, every living being who chooses to be born will experience aging, sickness, and death. In the interim, he or she also will experience loss, anxiety, pain, and affliction. We flee from these uncomfortable facts and run toward pleasurable activities, hoping to distract ourselves from unpleasantness. It's our denial of these basic facts, and our attempts to escape them through pleasurable pursuits, that produces stress in our lives. We hide from our suffering, thinking that we can find happiness in impermanent things, such as youth, sex, money, food, and drugs. But all of these things turn out to be disappointing and ephemeral. Furthermore, none of these escape strategies truly satisfies us. Like drinking salt water in an attempt to quench our thirst, we only become thirstier. Consequently, we run from pleasure to pleasure, always craving more. Our hearts long for something permanent and unchanging, a solid vessel to ferry us across the sea of existence. Some of us spend our entire lives chasing this phantom. We look to religion, philosophy, our parents, God, yearning for just a taste of eternal bliss. Paradoxically, we find that the more we chase happiness, the faster it runs away from us. Because of the elusive nature of happiness, many people fall into the belief that true contentment is impossible. This is why humankind suffers from a worldwide epidemic of ennui and despair.

We expect certain things from the people in our lives. We expect them to always be there for us, to always love us unconditionally, to never change. We want the euphoria of early love to last for the rest of our days. When it doesn't, we feel that we've lost something precious, that our lives have plunged into a dark tunnel.

Our problem is that we mistake the temporary satisfaction of our cravings for true happiness. We see a new car, for example, and we instantly want it. If we don't have it, we pine for it, and if we do buy it, we find that our pleasure in this shiny new toy is short-lived. The car ages, we grow tired of it, or it's destroyed in a wreck. Like a child, we grow bored with the new plaything and toss it aside in favor of something else. We crave a youthful and healthy body, but we find that both youth and health are impossible to hold on to. We see someone we find attractive, and we yearn for the person. We feel in the depths of our hearts that if we could only possess this desired other, we would find that eternal state of bliss for which we so desperately ache.

In our search for contentment, we're convinced that if we could find the right person, we would be happy forever. We crave undying and unconditional love, and when we don't have it, we suffer dreadfully. If we do find a life partner, we find that his or her good qualities are mixed with some damned annoying ones. We find that we've traded single-person stress for married-person stress. We feel let down, that the other person has failed us somehow. Or perhaps we failed ourselves. At any rate, our happiness, previously so intense and intoxicating, fades away. This tendency to seek permanence where there is none has existed as long as there have been people to seek it. This is no small matter. If we step back and take a look at the results of this universal unhappiness, we become aware of an astonishing fact: all of humankind's activities—science, medicine, psychology, religion, entertainment, war, and everything else we pursue—result from our valiant, and ultimately futile, efforts to find a permanent cure for this existential malady.

So what is the answer? Is true happiness possible? Yes, but it takes work. Whenever a person comes to me with a problem, my main strategy is finding out where this schism between expectations versus reality exists. If I can find that primal conflict, then I know I can help resolve it. Reality isn't always pleasant, but it's what we've got, and all the wishing in the world won't make it go away. We have to learn to deal with existence on its own terms. By no means does this mean that we should all become pessimists, forever expecting the worst. On the contrary, the more we face up to the sometimes-happy, sometimes-harsh nature of reality, the happier we become. When we set aside the craving for happiness, we find that the natural state of our mind, once freed from addictive craving, is relaxed, calm, and blissful. In other words, we're already happy; we just don't know it. We have to learn to get out of our own way.

When we accept the essential impermanence of all things, we learn two valuable lessons: (1) to appreciate to the fullest the good qualities of our lives in the present, and (2) to recognize that all the negative and horrible things in our lives will pass. We realize that life is short, that time passes quickly, and that taking the good with the bad is the best part of life. We learn freedom, because the harder we try to hold on to something, the more it eludes us. We learn to let stuff go, and by doing so it becomes ours forever.

People consult with me on a variety of problems, most of which result from an inner conflict between the life they want versus the life they have. I know that if I can find the source of this conflict, the dichotomy between what the person wants versus what he or she actually has, then I've taken an important step toward resolving the conflict. If people come to me and the source of their unhappiness is an abusive relationship, then I know that somewhere inside they are holding on to the belief that the other person will change if only they love the person enough. If people come to me because they hate their job, then I know that they feel that their happiness might be found in some other profession. What most of us forget is that happiness isn't something that can be found outside of ourselves. We have to find it within us, and this is something that we're not taught in school. Sometimes we need to be reminded how wonderful we are. We have within us a godlike power to shape our own lives, but it's pretty easy to forget this. Happy people didn't get that way by undertaking a lifelong quest for the Holy Grail of happiness. They're happy because they're engaged in activities that they feel happy doing, such as gardening, playing music, spending time with grandchildren, or writing a book. Happiness, like love itself, is an activity, not a feeling.

We create further confusion when we blame others for our emotional reactions. When someone does something we don't like, we say that the person "made us mad," or if we're in a bad mood, it's because we watched the evening news and decided that the world is going to the dogs. If we're totally honest with ourselves, then we'll admit that we made ourselves mad because the other person did something we didn't want them to do, or because the world isn't the perfect fairy tale place that we wish it would be. By taking control of our emotional reactions, we automatically reduce most of the frustration we experience toward the actions of other people. As John Milton reminds us in *Paradise Lost*, "The mind is its own place, and in itself can make a heaven of hell, a hell of heaven."

If we're to find true happiness, we have to look within ourselves and find a solid center, a secure and happy place from which we cannot be moved. We find, if we do this, that we're in complete control of our feelings. We've liberated our minds from the helter-skelter nature of the world around us. Furthermore—and most importantly—we find that we've taken complete control of our emotional states. This is a revelation both exhilarating and frightening: *I and only I am responsible for my feelings. I cannot control how another person acts, but I have total control over my reactions to what other people say and do to me. I am the cause of my karma, the heir to my karma, and the agent of my karma; not fate, not God, not the government, not other people: Me.* This message has been taught since primordial days by messiahs and philosophers, but it seems to be a message we're reluctant to hear. However, the instant I got this through my thick head, my life became infinitely better.

It's not possible to have a happy relationship with another person if you're unhappy with yourself. When our minds are relaxed, happy, and free, we're satisfied to be by ourselves, keeping our own company. If we don't like ourselves, how can we expect anyone else to like us? Just as happiness eludes us the more we chase it, so does frantically seeking the approval of others drive them away.

A relationship with another human being can't be based on the fantasies promulgated by top-forty love songs. We have to make an honest appraisal of who we are, what we're looking for in a relationship, and who the other person is. Once we figure all that out, we're better equipped to work with what we find. A perfect relationship exists only in our imagination. If we hold out for a perfect connection, we're going to sit alone on our couch for a long time. In spite of its undeniable attractions, the world is sometimes a hard place in which to live, but it seems easier when you walk through the travails and complications of life with a congenial partner holding your hand. I find that the objective insights gained through palmistry help us understand the strengths and weaknesses of our potential mate. Once we truly know someone and accept him or her without expectations, we find that forgiveness and tolerance arise naturally.

I'll climb down from my soapbox now and we'll get back to our investigation of how palmistry can help us find that congenial hand to hold. The following profiles concisely describe some romantic archetypes and the common palmistry traits for each type of lover.

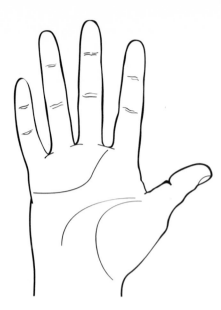

Figure 7–1: Romantic lover hand

Romantic Lover

Look for an air, water, or conic hand with a curved heart line, the longer the better. The head line curves downward toward the heel of the hand. There should be a large mount of Venus and a wide, sweeping Venusian line. The little finger (Mercury) should curve inward toward Apollo, and there should be a wide space between the heart line and head line. The plain of Mars (the center of the palm) should be concave, like a cup.

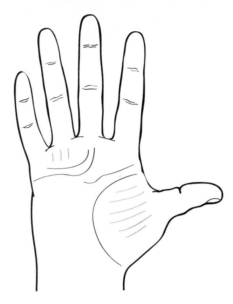

Figure 7-2: Sensitive lover hand

Sensitive Lover

Look for a water, psychic, or conic hand with a long, curved heart line ending under the second finger (Saturn). A girdle of Venus adds extra empathy. A medium-length, straight head line adds a balance between logic and intuition. The little finger (Mercury) curves toward the third finger (Apollo). Worry lines on the mount of Venus show a concern for the welfare of loved ones. Other lines to look for are nurse's lines (vertical lines between the heart line and fingers), which are an indication of a sensitive and empathic touch. The thumb should be flexible, bending back forty-five to ninety degrees in relation to the rest of the hand. The middle phalange (Athena) of the thumb should be wasp-waisted in the middle.

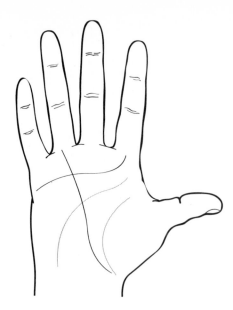

Figure 7-3: Imaginative lover hand

Imaginative Lover

Look for an air, fire, or philosophic hand with a long, curved heart line; a long, curved head line; a line of Apollo; or a large Apollo mount. The third finger (Apollo) is longer than the first finger (Jupiter). The little finger (Mercury) curves toward the third finger (Apollo). The angle of the thumb should approach ninety degrees, showing a mind open to new, novel ideas.

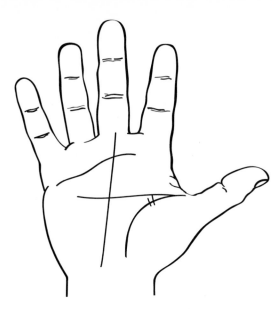

Figure 7-4: Realistic lover hand

Realistic Lover

Look for an earth or metal hand, or possibly a wood hand if it contains a long, straight head line. There should be a gently curved or straight heart line. The angle of the thumb should be greater than forty-five degrees but not a full ninety degrees. Look for a straight heart line and a Venusian line that is closer to the thumb than the outer edge of the hand. A long middle finger (Saturn) coupled with a long Saturn line running the length of the palm shows a practical approach. Both the upper and lower Mars mounts should be firm but not too hard.

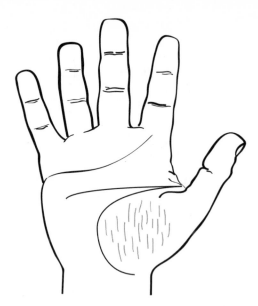

Figure 7-5: Dominant lover hand

Dominant Lover

Look for a fire, a metal, or sometimes an earth hand. Signs of a dominant nature include a long, rigid thumb with rounded end, and a long first finger (Jupiter). The Jupiter mount should be large and ruddy in color. The angle of the thumb to the rest of the hand should be forty-five degrees or less. There should be a straight, medium-to-long head line. The heart line ends under the first finger (Apollo). Both the upper and lower Mars mounts are hard. The mount of Venus is large and hard and has several short, vertical lines across its width.

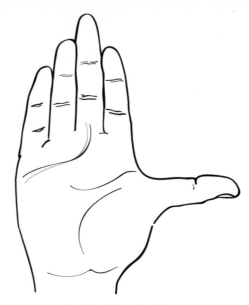

Figure 7-6: Submissive lover hand

Submissive Lover

Look for an air, water, conic, or psychic hand with an extremely flexible thumb and a long, curved heart line ending under the second finger (Saturn) or extending into the second finger. In a truly submissive person, there may be a faint secondary heart line, creating a double heart line. The angle of the thumb should be ninety degrees or greater. There should be a short index finger (Jupiter) and a low or missing Saturn mount. The head line is short and curved. Both the upper and lower Mars mounts are spongy.

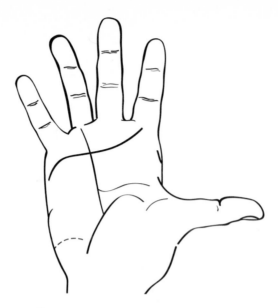

Figure 7-7: Kinky lover hand

Kinky Lover

Look for a fire, air, crescent, or spatulate hand with a long, curved heart line. There should be a short- to medium-length, curved head line. An Apollo line, and/or the third finger (Apollo) curved toward the little finger (Mercury), adds creative imagination and a desire to express it. There is a strong but flexible thumb with a long first phalange (Rhea) that bends back at least ninety degrees. The thumb base should be low-set, showing spontaneity and an unconventional approach to sex. The little finger (Mercury) is angled away from the hand, with a large mount of Mercury or wavy Mercury line. A large, ruddy mount of Venus and a long, wide Venusian line should be present. The via lascivia, preferably attached to a Mercury line, adds a strong libido and a love for sexual variety. The Mars mounts are firm but not hard.

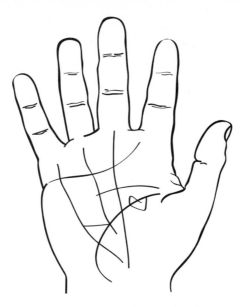

Figure 7-8: Good provider hand

Good Provider

Look for an earth or metal hand with a medium-length heart line and a long, firm thumb with a long middle phalange (Athena). When held naturally, the fingers should be close together, with no gaps between them. The head line has a gentle curve. A narrow angle between the thumb and the rest of the hand shows a rigid focus on goals and a strong loyalty to one's personal values. Other details include a Mercury line and/or an Apollo line, and a Saturn line that spans the length of the hand. Triangles on the Venusian line indicate periods of financial windfall. The upper Mars mount should be firm and well-rounded.

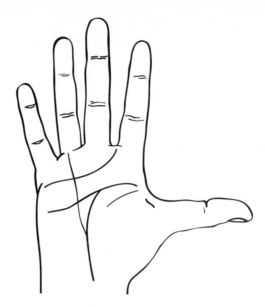

Figure 7-9: Refined tastes hand

Lover with Refined Tastes

If you want someone who shares your love of art, literature, movies, and fine foods, then look for an air, water, wood, or conic hand with the following details: a long third finger (Apollo) with a well-developed Apollo mount, and a long second finger (Saturn). A wide angle between the thumb and the rest of the hand, at least ninety degrees or more, shows an open mind and love for cultural variety. A long, curved heart line paired with a long, straight head line shows both emotional sensitivity and intellectual appreciation of cultural matters. A Venusian line exactly in the middle of the palm shows a balance between the desire for a well-rooted home life and the urge to travel to interesting places.

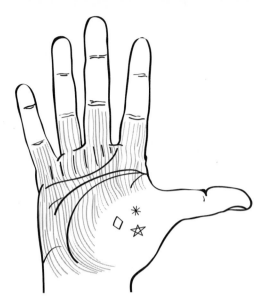

Figure 7-10: Good in bed hand

Good in Bed

To determine if your potential lover is skilled in bed, look primarily at the mount of Venus and the Venusian line. Check for a well-rounded and ruddy mount of Venus with a star or a diamond on it; a wide, sweeping Venusian line with few breaks; and few lines in the Venus area. Worry lines can drain Venus's energy, leaving the person too emotionally drained to show much interest in sex. Water and earth hands are skilled at erotic touch and foreplay, while fire and metal are aggressive and demanding lovers. Air and wood are inventive and curious sexual partners. Nurse's lines show a sensitive, empathic touch that can find all the erogenous areas. A wide angle between the thumb and the rest of the hand, at least ninety degrees or more, shows an open mind and a love for sexual variety. A curved heart line, especially one that ends between the first and second fingers, shows a tender and constant lover. A forked head line is a good sign, as it indicates both good technique and an imaginative mind. If you desire an insatiable and expressive lover but not necessarily an emotional commitment, look for the via lascivia.

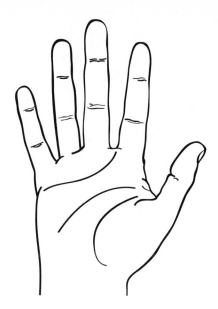

Figure 7-11: Generous lover hand

Generous Lover

Earth, metal, and wood tend to be cautious spenders, while fire and air see money as a means to an end and will spend it freely. When the hand is held naturally with the fingers widespread, it's a sign that the person is generous—sometimes too generous—with money. A wide gap between the head line and heart line adds to the generosity. A long, sweeping heart line makes it likely that the person will lavish you with romantic gifts.

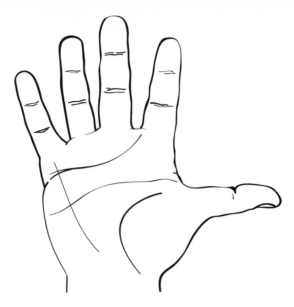

Figure 7-12: Communicative lover hand

Good Communicator

Wood and air are the best verbal communicators, with earth a close second. Wood and air express their views and feelings, while earth's communication skills tend to be down-to-earth and practical. Mercury represents the expression of communication, so look for a long, straight little finger (Mercury); a Mercury line; and/or a well-developed Mercury mount. I also suggest looking for a wide angle to the thumb, which shows an appreciation for different views, opinions, and experiences. A fork at the beginning of the heart line (near the heel of the hand) shows a friendly disposition and a love of conversation.

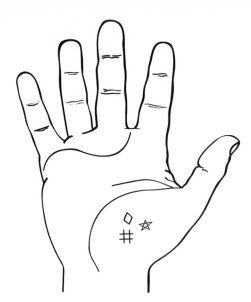

Figure 7-13: Passionate lover hand

Passionate Lover

Look for an earth, fire, wood, or action hand with square fingernails, a deeply curved heart line that runs close to the fingers, and a short head line. A star or diamond on the mount of Venus shows skills in the bedroom. Crosshatches on Venus show an extremely passionate lover. Square fingernails show the desire to please one's lover. There should be a wide space between the head line and heart line.

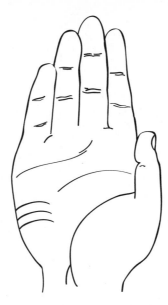

Figure 7-14: Active lover hand

Active and Energetic Lover

Obviously, the action hand is the one to look for, although water and fire hands are active and busy too. The hand should be warm and firm to the touch. Both the head line and the heart line are curved and medium length. The fingers should have round tips, and the thumb is short and rounded at the tip. The tip of the thumb (Rhea) is shorter than the middle phalange (Athena). An Apollo line is an optional but desirable feature. Travel lines on Luna and a forked Venusian line show a desire to be active and to travel. A well-developed Mercury mount and long Mercury finger add charm and verbal spontaneity. All of the Mars areas are firm and flexible.

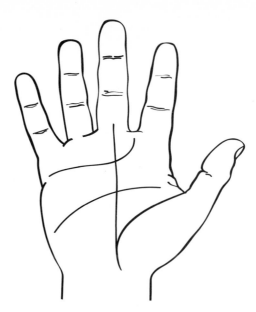

Figure 7-15: Faithful lover hand

Faithful or Fickle Lover?

Earth, metal, and wood tend to be the most faithful lovers, as loyal as old hound dogs (figure 7-15). Air and fire, due to their love of spontaneous thrills and variety, are the most common strayers, but not necessarily. Since water types follow their heart in love, they can be either faithful or fickle depending on the circumstances. When in love, water can be deeply faithful, but if the lovers drift apart emotionally, water can lose his or her heart to someone else. A solid, smoothly curved and unbroken heart line is a good sign. Also look for a long, straight middle finger (Saturn) as a sign of moral firmness. A long, firm thumb and a long, straight Saturn line show someone who doesn't give in to temptation. Usually, the faithful and honest person has a firm but not crushing hand grip.

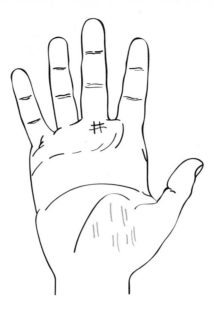

Figure 7-16: Fickle lover hand

Breaks and tatters in the heart line can show emotional irregularities, so they are a warn-ing sign of a fickle lover, as is a lack of a Saturn mound or crosshatching under Saturn (fig-ure 7-16). Examine Venus for several short, vertical lines. If there are many, the person will be tempted to cheat when younger, but eventually will settle down. A triangle on Venus denotes a love triangle, so the person might find sexual gratification only when two lov-ers are in his or her life. Forked attachment lines show a fickle tendency. A short forefinger (Jupiter) can indicate someone who bolsters low self-esteem through sexual conquest. Both the upper and lower Mars mounts are large but spongy. The thumb is smaller than average. The person's grip is weak, and he or she avoids a prolonged handshake.

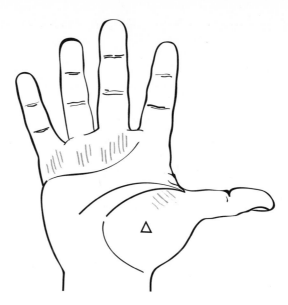

Figure 7-17: Good parent hand

Good Parent

Although no hand element in and of itself is considered an indication of a bad parent, earth and water types tend to be the most nurturing parents. On any hand, look for a lot of children lines. The more children lines a person has, the more nurturing he or she is to all living creatures. Capacity for love is seen in a long heart line. A firm upper Mars mount equals a firm hand in disciplining children—tough but fair. The presence of nurse's lines shows a soothing hand that calms upset children and crying babies. Lines in Vulcan (the area of family aggravation) show that the person tends to worry about his or her loved ones.

chapter eight

You Try It!

The following are some hand prints from my collection. See if you can tell which couples are compatible and which are not, and what predictable issues each couple will have to confront in the relationship.

Corinne and William

Let's look at the case of Corinne and William (figures 8-1 and 8-2). Looking at their palms, consider the following questions:

- Are the elements compatible?
- What do the heart lines tell us?
- Do the two think alike?
- Who is more stubborn?
- Are they on the same page concerning money?

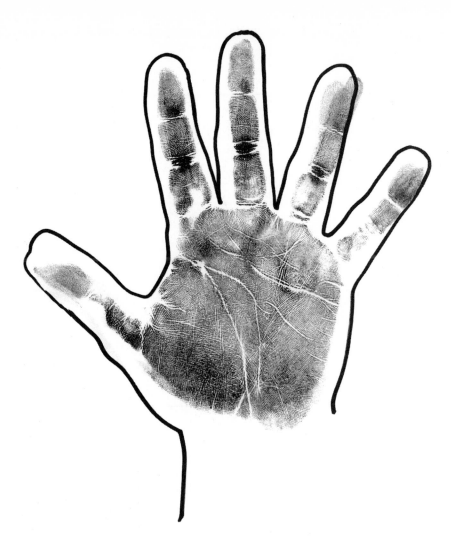

Figure 8-1: Corinne

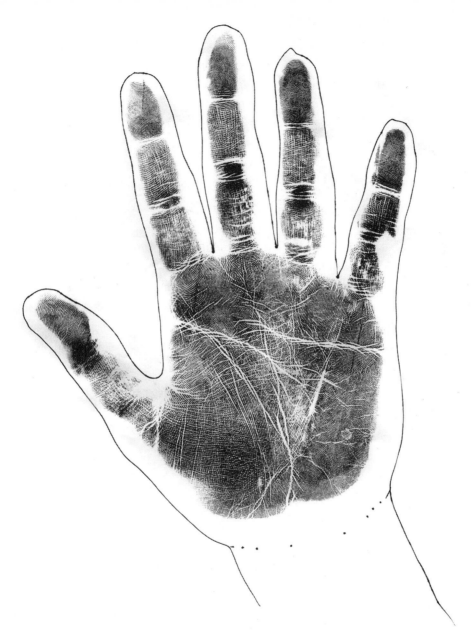

Figure 8-2: William

Corinne and William are compatible elements: earth and water, respectively. In terms of money, earth likes to save for security, and water values security and will compromise for the sake of the future.

Corinne has a medium-length, physical heart line, so she's more taciturn than William, who has a broad, sweeping physical heart line. Corinne will be delighted at the excellent foot and back rubs that William's nurse's lines promise, as well as his powerful sex drive, which she shares (both have large mounts of Venus). Corinne's Venusian line is close to her thumb, so she'll probably settle down to be a homebody, while William has a restless nature due to his wide Venusian line. I see Corinne as a stay-at-home mom with a business that she runs out of the home, probably involving crafts or art of some kind, or possibly writing. William has the hand of a motivated professional who will seek a career that's reliable and stable and provides a good income with good benefits.

Both William and Corinne have a strong Jupiter finger, but Corinne's Jupiter challenges Saturn, so in a battle of wills she'll probably get her way. Both also have a firm thumb, so there will be a need to learn the skills of compromise. Notice the angle of both thumbs, each of which falls short of ninety degrees. Both individuals will be a bit critical, and feel more comfortable around people who share their own beliefs and opinions.

Corinne's head line shows an intense, creative nature, with a faint logical fork. Her creativity would express itself in very detailed, precise endeavors. William's head line is more logical and forks at the end. He has the mind of a lawyer or engineer, able to analyze things logically and communicate his findings to others.

Notice that both William and Corinne show independence in their Mercury fingers, which stick out at an angle from the hand. With their need for personal independence, these partners have to make sure they don't lose sight of the fact that they are an interdependent couple.

James and Hilda

Next, take a look at the palms of James and Hilda (figures 8-3 and 8-4) and consider the same set of questions:

- Are the elements compatible?

- What do the heart lines tell us?

- Do the two think alike?

- Who is more stubborn?

- Are they on the same page concerning money?

James is a fire and Hilda is a water. To be more specific, Hilda has a psychic hand. These elements are not complementary, so these partners have their work cut out for them. Even though the sex between them is passionate and intense, they will have to look for other, deeper reasons to stay together.

James has a physical heart line, which means he readily shows his emotions. Notice that he has several lines shooting off from the heart line, indicating he has a flirty nature and a roaming eye. Hilda's heart line shows an introspective nature, which can become sullen in the face of James's emotional outbursts. The many water lines on Hilda's hand shows her sensitivity to emotional states, and in the presence of James's intense fire energy, she will be high-strung and nervous.

Both James and Hilda have a Mercury line, so their communication skills are excellent—just maybe not with each other. Fire and water have different approaches to life and to love, so James and Hilda speak totally different languages.

Both have practical head lines, so they can apply reason and logic to their differences. Hilda's head line shows a trident, which means she is remarkably receptive to different points of view. This is one factor that can help save this otherwise problematical match. Both show a forked Venusian line, so they share a love of travel. Both also have a large mount of Venus, which hints to me that they came together through a mutually powerful sexual attraction.

James's thumb is short and stubborn, while Hilda's is long and flexible, with a wasp-shaped Athena that reveals a diplomatic nature. She will tend to keep her opinions to herself in a passive manner, but will seem to get her way in the end through sheer endurance. Notice that Hilda's Mercury shows an independent spirit. James's fire nature, quick and impulsive, will give in to her quiet determination over time. Her Jupiter is longer in relation to Apollo than James's, so although he blusters and shouts, she really is the one in control in this relationship.

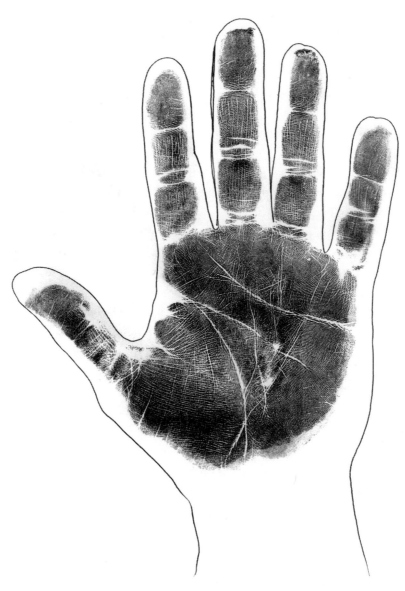

Figure 8-3: James

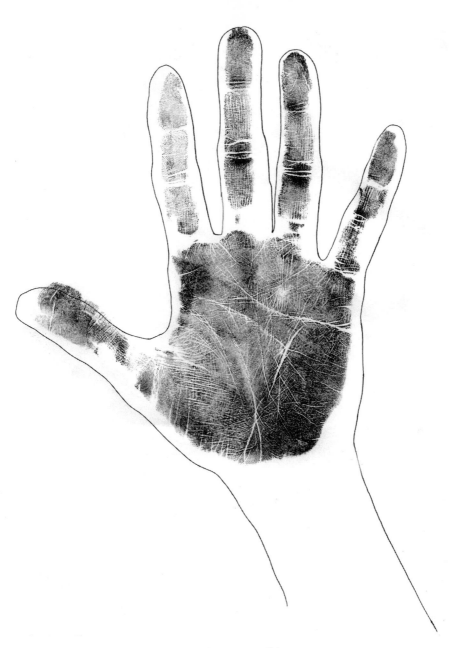

Figure 8-4: Hilda

Conclusion

This book was five years in the writing, much longer than I had expected when I began the project. Life can be unpredictable, and as Robert Burns assures us, even the best plans of mice and men "gang aft a-gley."[1]

There were many reasons for this delay. During the five-year interim I experienced the breakup of a marriage, the death of my mother, and an eventual remarriage (which came as a complete surprise; a friendship turned into something deeper while I was day-dreaming about something else) and relocation to a different part of the country. I found that these experiences forced me to reexamine my preconceived notions about relationships. I also deepened my commitment to Buddhism, which gave me a fuller understanding of the impermanent nature of existence and increased insight into the nuts and bolts of true happiness.

---

1 *To a Mouse, on Turning Her Up in Her Nest with the Plough*, 1785.

Adding texture to this tapestry of interesting experiences were the capricious and seemingly malicious actions of my computer. I lost this book twice, once by accident and once through the unexplainable destruction of two hard drives and two backup floppy disks. It was as though the book didn't want to be written. Perhaps something was telling me that I was on the wrong track. I discarded my previous approaches and began again from scratch. This time the writing of the book went easily and without further incident. Looking back, I think that, through several concurrent fortunate fruitings of karma, I was granted the information I needed to make this book useful and coherent. So I hope with all my heart that the information in this book helps you find happiness and contentment, whether you're in a relationship or just trying to learn to get along with yourself—which, as I have learned, can be the hardest task of all.

As we part company, I would like to leave you with one of the most beautiful and poignant anecdotes in Buddhist literature, concerning a married couple who were truly in love. This is my condensed retelling of the Samajivina Sutta from the Anguttara Nikaya:[2]

> Once the Buddha was staying in the Deer Park at Bhesakala Grove, near Crocodile Haunt. One of Buddha's disciples was a young man named Nakula, and early one morning Buddha put on his robes and went to the home of Nakula's father. Nakula's father and mother went to the Buddha, bowed down to him, and sat to one side. Nakula's father said, "Lord, ever since Nakula's mother was brought to be my wife when I was a young boy, I have never been unfaithful to her even in my mind, much less in body. We want to be together not only in the present life but also in our future life."
>
> Nakula's mother said to the Buddha, "Lord, ever since I was brought to Nakula's father to be his wife when I was just a young girl, I have never been unfaithful to him even in mind, much less in body. We want to be together not only in the present life but also in our future life."
>
> The Buddha responded, "If a husband and wife want be together not only in the present life but also in the life to come, they should be in tune with each other in conviction, in virtue, in generosity, and in discernment. Then they will surely see one another not only in the present life but also in the life to come."

---

2 Bhikkhu Nanamoli, *A Translation of the Anguttara Nikaya,* sutta 4.5.

He went on: "Husband and wife, both living with conviction, being responsive, being restrained, living by the Dharma (the truth as Buddha taught it), addressing each other with loving words, will benefit in many diverse ways. Happiness comes to them. Their enemies are dejected when both are in tune in values and virtue. Having followed the Truth here in this world, both together in tune in precepts and practices, they delight together in heaven, enjoying whatever pleasures they want."

May you be at peace, may you be free from stress and the causes of stress, and may you find the person with whom you are in perfect tune.

Jon Saint-Germain
February 14, 2007

Bibliography

Bailey, Allison A., and Peter L. Hurd. "Finger Length Ratio (2D:4D) Correlates with Physical Aggression in Men but Not in Women." *Biological Psychology* 68, no. 3 (March 2005).

———. *A Translation of the Majjhima Nikaya*. Somerville, MA: Wisdom Publications, 1995.

Cheiro (Count Louis Hamon). *Palmistry for All*. New York: Arco, 1982.

Gettings, Fred. *The Book of the Hand*. London: Hamlyn, 1965.

———. *The Hand and the Horoscope*. London: Triune Books, 1974.

Gibson, Litzka R. *How to Read Palms*. Hollywood, FL: Lifetime Books, 1997.

Nanamoli, Bhikkhu. *A Translation of the Anguttara Nikaya*. Somerville, MA: Wisdom Publications, 1995.

Saint-Germain, Jon. *Karmic Palmistry*. St. Paul, MN: Llewellyn Publications, 2003.

———. *Runic Palmistry*. St. Paul, MN: Llewellyn Publications, 2001.

Webster, Richard. *Revealing Hands*. St. Paul, MN: Llewellyn Publications, 1994.

Index

To Write to the Author

If you wish to contact the author or would like more information about this book, please write to the author in care of Llewellyn Worldwide and we will forward your request. Both the author and publisher appreciate hearing from you and learning of your enjoyment of this book and how it has helped you. Llewellyn Worldwide cannot guarantee that every letter written to the author can be answered, but all will be forwarded. Please write to:

Jon Saint-Germain
℅ Llewellyn Worldwide
2143 Wooddale Drive, Dept. 978-0-7387-1280-2
Woodbury, Minnesota 55125-2989, U.S.A.

Please enclose a self-addressed stamped envelope for reply,
or $1.00 to cover costs. If outside U.S.A., enclose
international postal reply coupon.

Many of Llewellyn's authors have websites with additional information and resources. For more information, please visit our website at http://www.llewellyn.com.

LLEWELLYN ORDERING INFORMATION

Runic Palmistry
A Norse Method of Divination

JON SAINT-GERMAIN

This unique book combines standard palmistry, Norse mythology, and the runes, using all three to understand a person and his or her path, personality, needs and special gifts.

It is a system handed down orally through four generations of Jon Saint-Germain's family, originally learned from a mysterious Scandinavian who entered the family circle two hundred years ago. In this system, lines of the palm are called "branches," and mounts of the palm are named after Norse deities. You will learn the meanings of the fingers in the light of exciting Norse mythology. This is the only book on the subject available.

1-56718-577-0, 240 pp., 7½ x 9⅛   **$14.95**

Palm Reading for Beginners

Find the Future in the Palm of Your Hand

RICHARD WEBSTER

Announce in any gathering that you read palms and you will be flocked by people thrilled to show you their hands. When you have finished *Palm Reading for Beginners*, you will be able to look at anyone's palm (including your own) and confidently and effectively tell them about their personality, love life, hidden talents, career options, prosperity, and health.

Palmistry is possibly the oldest of the occult sciences, with basic principles that have not changed in 2,600 years. This step-by-step guide clearly explains the basics, as well as advanced research conducted in the past few years on such subjects as dermatoglyphics.

1-56718-791-9, 264 pp., 5³⁄₁₆ x 8   **$12.95**

To order, call 1-877-NEW-WRLD

Prices subject to change without notice

Instant Palm Reader

A Road Map to Life

LINDA DOMIN

Etched upon your palm is an aerial view of all the scenes you will travel in the course of your lifetime. Your characteristics, skills, and abilities are imprinted in your mind and transferred as images on to your hand. Now, with this simple, flip-through pictorial guide, you can assemble your own personal palm reading, like a professional, almost instantly.

The *Instant Palm Reader* shows you how your hands contain the picture of the real you—physically, emotionally, and mentally. More than 500 easy-to-read diagrams will provide you with candid, uplifting revelations about yourself: personality, childhood, career, finances, family, love life, talents, and destiny.

With the sensitive information artfully contained within each interpretation, you will also be able to uncover your hidden feelings and unconscious needs as you learn the secrets of this 3,000-year-old science.

1–56718–232–1, 256 pp., 7 x 10 **$16.95**

To order, call 1-877-NEW-WRLD
Prices subject to change without notice

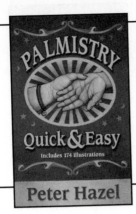

Palmistry Quick & Easy

Peter Hazel

Gain instant access to this ancient science. *Palmistry Quick & Easy* brings new millennium awareness and interpretations to centuries of traditional knowledge of palmistry. The innovative interactive format leads you through 232 different questions and 170 illustrations designed to give you perceptive insight into the deepest motivations of yourself and others.

Experienced palmists will also find this book to be a useful and concise reference, neatly divided into the traditional categories: length of the palm and fingers, the four hand types, thumbs, marks on fingers, the lines, fingernails, the mounts, timing in the palm, and even the meaning of rings.

1–56718–410–3, 288 pp. 5³⁄₁₆ x 8   **$9.95**

To order, call 1-877-NEW-WRLD

Prices subject to change without notice

Magical Symbols
of Love & Romance

RICHARD WEBSTER

A candlelight dinner, wine, and roses are obvious choices when you want to woo a special someone. But this is only the tip of a colossal heart-shaped iceberg when it comes to expressing love and creating romance.

From pearls to pomegranates, tulips to truffles, vodka to Venus, Richard Webster introduces a wide array of items that signify this ubiquitous, complicated emotion. Going back to prehistoric cave paintings, Greek and Roman myth, and the origin of Valentine's Day, he offers a colorful history of love rituals, spells, charms, and aphrodisiacs. Modern success stories illustrate how individuals have used these powerful symbols to attract a partner, stimulate marriage, or resolve relationship issues. A handy reference and practical guide rolled into one, this book also advises on how to use these symbols in your own life.

0-7387-1032-6, 264 pp., 5³⁄₁₆ x 8

$12.95